Oryx American Family Tree Series

A Student's Guide to
POLISH AMERICAN
Genealogy

By Carl Sokolnicki Rollyson and
Lisa Olson Paddock

Oryx Press
1996

Copyright 1996 by The Rosen Publishing Group, Inc.
Published in 1996 by The Oryx Press
4041 North Central at Indian School Road
Phoenix, Arizona 85012-3397

Printed and bound in the United States of America

∞ The paper used in this publication meets the minimum
requirements of American National Standard for Information
Science—Permanence of Paper for Printed Library Materials,
ANSI Z39.48, 1984.

Library of Congress Cataloging-in-Publication Data
Rollyson, Carl Sokolnicki.
   A student's guide to Polish-American genealogy / Carl Sokolnicki
Rollyson, Lisa Olson Paddock.
      p.   cm. — (Oryx American family tree series)
   Includes bibliographical references and index.
   ISBN 0-89774-974-X
   1. Polish Americans—Genealogy—Handbooks, manuals, etc.
2. Polish Americans—Genealogy—Bibliography.   I. Paddock, Lisa
Olson.   II. Title.   III. Series: Oryx American family tree.
E184.P7R65   1996
929'.1'0899185—dc20   95-41416
                                                                 CIP

Contents

Chapter 1
Tracing Your Roots

Sooner or later most people become curious about their roots. Perhaps an important member of the family dies. People remember stories that he or she told about the family. The family wants to know more. Perhaps a distant cousin visits for the first time and brings fascinating anecdotes about relatives. Everyone, every family, has stories to tell, adventures to be relived. Each generation treasures memories of a family's journey through life; but each generation also forgets. Searching for roots helps preserve and even expand a family's story. While individuals find out about their families, they also discover aspects of themselves.

If you are descended from Polish immigrants, you are one of millions of people who share a part in the building of modern America. Learning about Poland and Polish Americans will mean discovering fascinating things about your neighbors, your community, or your own family.

By definition, a descendant of immigrants inherits the stories of a whole people forging a new identity in a new land. Many family members know parts of the immigration story. The great challenge is to assemble the historical record. The rewards will be many: presenting your family with a story to which everyone has contributed and yet which no one knows as fully as you do; learning a great deal about Polish and American history and the history of immigration; becoming a practiced researcher.

Constructing a family history is almost like writing a historical novel. Along the way, you are likely to formulate several intriguing questions. Why did some members of the family leave Poland while others stayed? What communication was there between the "old country" and the United

Polish immigrants had to wait to have their papers processed after enduring the long trip to the United States. Here, a Polish mother and her eight children await entry into their new country.

States? What did your ancestors expect to find? Were they satisfied or surprised by this country? Did your relatives visit Poland after leaving it? Your family history may also be a kind of mystery story. You may be seeking information about your birth parents rather than your current household members. Or you may simply want to know more about the stories you have heard your parents and grandparents tell.

To understand Polish immigrants, you need to know something about the history of Poland and about that part of it from which your family members came. Chapter 2 provides a brief history of the "old country" and suggests further reading about Polish culture and its outstanding figures.

Don't overlook the very rich tradition of Polish literature or contemporary events in Poland. The more you know about Poland—your parents' country—the more you discover what makes you Polish American.

Your opinions about your family, community, and country

may change as you explore the nature of what it means to be a Polish American. You will probably become interested in comparing the experiences of Polish Americans with those of other immigrant groups. At the end of this chapter the **Resources** section lists several books that provide an insight into immigrant history, followed by a section specifically on the Polish immigrant experience.

People who have done family histories and genealogical searches (efforts to trace their direct ancestors and their families) often discover relatives who can serve as role models. Their stories may be nearly as remarkable as that of General John Shalikashvili, the son of a Polish mother and Georgian father who was appointed by President Clinton to be the first foreign-born chair of the Joint Chiefs of Staff. General Shalikashvili first came to prominence during the 1991 Persian Gulf War when he commanded Operation Provide Comfort.

General Shalikashvili represents the immigrant experience in all its complexity. He came to this country as a political refugee from war-ravaged Poland. At the Senate hearings called to consider his appointment as chair of the Joint Chiefs, it was revealed that his father, a Georgian nationalist who had fought against Joseph Stalin's Red Army, had been an officer in an elite Nazi military group associated with the Waffen SS (this was after he could no longer serve in the Polish Army, which was crushed by Hitler in September 1939). General Shalikashvili explained that he had been a child during the Warsaw Uprising in 1944, running through the sewers as the city above was bombed and his own apartment building collapsed.

In his case, the immigrant story has become not only a success story but a reckoning with a dark past—although Shalikashvili does not believe his father shared the Nazi ideology.

As you study the lives of Polish Americans, you will be astonished to see how rapidly they have adopted and adapted to their new land. But family setbacks and tragedies may be just as moving and instructive as successes, helping

These two young peasant women are representative of many Polish immigrants who came to the United States with only the belongings they could carry.

Polish Americans formed large communities in cities such as Pittsburgh, Detroit, Chicago, and Buffalo. In 1927, this corner of Milwaukee Avenue and Division Street in Chicago was in the heart of "Little Poland."

to put into perspective your own worries and disappointments. We are always assimilating new experiences and adjusting to our culture; the immigrant experience can be looked on as a particularly intense version of identity-formation and adjustment to society, in which immigrants have helped to change the United States for the better because they have not been content with things as they are. Indeed, it has been argued that immigrants have kept this a dynamic country, eager to pursue new ways of doing things.

The United States has been called the "first universal nation." What part has the Polish American family played in a country built by so many different ethnic groups? Polish Americans are currently among the ten most numerous ancestry groups in the United States. This means that your family's history is likely to reflect the country's tremendous variety and complexity; your family's history will be representative in many important respects, a kind of United States in miniature.

More than 2 million Poles immigrated to the growing U.S. cities after 1880. Polish Americans are part of the urban experience, having established large communities in Pittsburgh, Detroit, Chicago, and Buffalo.

The bulk of Polish immigration to the United States occurred at a time when Poland was partitioned by the neighboring countries of Germany, Russia, and Austria. Most of the immigrants from German-occupied Poland came from relatively urban areas and had experience working in factories and mines, so they had a fairly smooth transition to life in urban and industrial centers of the United States. Poles from Russian-occupied Poland also tended to be industrial workers. Poles who immigrated from Austrian-occupied Galicia, by contrast, were predominantly agricultural laborers. Economic reasons were the primary cause of Polish immigration to the United States between 1870 and 1914, according to James S. Pula in *Polish Americans: An Ethnic Community* (see **Resources**). Wages in the United States were many times higher than those in Poland.

Even though many Polish immigrants had been agricultural workers in Poland, after coming to the United States the vast majority took jobs in factories in urban areas. Some immigrants continued to pursue agriculture, mostly in Michigan, Wisconsin, Illinois, and Indiana. New England and the Middle Atlantic states became home to Polish immigrants who worked as miners.

By tracing your family's roots you will also relive the history of industrialism in this country. You will learn how your family members got jobs; you will also gain some insight into changes in the U.S. economy and the hardships and new challenges facing immigrants today.

Your research will be anything but dry and boring. You may discover new photographs of relatives and of places where your family lived that will make your quest for facts come to life. You may see in a picture features like your own—but they may date from 1910 or 1920; it will feel as if you are holding the past in your hands—especially if the

Studying about your family's history may deepen your appreciation of the experience of Polish immigrants like Isaac and Ida Block of Vilna, Poland, who sought better lives in the United States.

pictures become part of interviews, oral histories, and other tools you will use to make the past live again.

You will become adept at reading maps, securing documents such as birth and death certificates and military records, and using many kinds of reference works. You will find many helpers—in public libraries and archives, in genealogical societies, and of course among members of your own family. Like a good detective, you will learn on the job. You will make your share of mistakes, but you can pace yourself, backtracking when necessary. Do not be afraid to reinterview people, to reread the materials you collect. Veteran researchers will tell you that everyone goes through the same trial-and-error process. This book offers many pointers on how to organize your research, but you will also experience the joy of developing your own methods.

Keep your goal constantly in mind: You are on a journey of self-discovery. What you find is important to you. You may find family members who are initially reluctant to talk or skeptical of your project, saying they have no worthwhile information for you. Don't give up! Encourage your sources to speak up, even when they doubt they can help you. How you handle yourself will have an enormous impact on the people you interview. If they see you are interested, they are likely to share your enthusiasm.

In a way, searching for your Polish roots—or helping a friend to do so—is a reenactment of the immigrant experience, which itself was a journey, a quest for a better life, a way to express the self. Although you cannot actually relive the immigrant experience, your desire to understand it is a kind of reenactment of your ancestors' adventure. You have the benefit of looking backward; in this sense you have the potential to know more than the people you study, for they could not know exactly what they would face once ashore in the United States. You are ashore and can look back at the cumulative record of the past, the buildup of history.

Listed below are books that will help you get started thinking about your roots and the place of Polish Americans in the history of U.S. immigration. Take inspiration from the stories of others. Read some of the autobiographies, oral histories, historical and biographical studies. They will give you an idea of form—what a genealogical study or family history can look like. They should give you inspiration and provide you with working models. Once you have a grounding in historical, biographical, and genealogical research—and after you master the basic history of Poland—you will be able to create your own history and to act as your own guide to your Polish American past, present, and future.

Resources

STARTING YOUR EXPLORATION

Bailey, Sproule. *Poland.* **Austin, TX: Raintree Steck Vaughn, 1991.**

An illustrated overview of the Polish land and people.

Greene, Carol. *Marie Curie: Pioneer Physicist.* **Chicago: Children's Press, 1984.**

An illustrated biography of the Polish scientific pioneer.

———. *Poland.* **Chicago: Children's Press, 1983.**

A photo-illustrated look at the geography, history, economics, and key attractions of Poland. Includes brief biographies of major figures and a "quick facts" section.

Hautzig, Esther. *The Endless Steppe: Growing Up in Siberia.* **New York: HarperCollins/Crowell, 1968.**

A personal account of the author's years as a Polish deportee in a Siberian village during World War II.

Pfeiffer, Christine. *Poland: Land of Freedom Fighters.* **Columbus, OH: Silver Burdett Press, 1991.**

Part of the Discovering Our Heritage series. Read about the geography, people, history, holidays, sports, school and family life of Poland.

Steinke, Ann. *Marie Curie and the Discovery of Radium.* **Chicago: Children's Press, 1988.**

Part of a Profiles in Science for Young People series.

Reilly, J. *Life & Works: Joseph Conrad.* **Vero Beach, FL: Rourke, 1990.**

Excerpts from the work of a Polish immigrant and famous writer and an explanation of how his work related to his life and events of his time.

Sharman, Tim. *The Rise of Solidarity.* **Vero Beach, FL: Rourke, 1987.**

Information on how Solidarity evolved, how it affected world affairs, and the issues it raised are addressed. Illustrated by drawings and photographs.

Singer, Isaac Bashevis. *The Certificate.* **New York: Farrar, Straus & Giroux, 1992.**

The story of an eighteen-year-old boy who moves to Warsaw from a small village.

Strom, Yale. *A Tree Still Stands: Jewish Youth in Eastern Europe Today.* **New York: Putnam/Philomel, 1990.**

Jewish youths from Poland and other countries tell their stories. Illustrated with photo essays.

IMMIGRANT HISTORY

"America's Challenge." *Time,* **Fall, 1993.**

A succinct history of immigration, the experiences of different ethnic groups, the changing attitudes of Americans toward immigration.

Appel, John J., ed. *The New Immigration.* **New York: Jerome S. Ozer, 1971.**

A collection of articles with chronology and a bibliographical essay.

Crevecoeur, J. Hector St. John de. *Letters from an American Farmer.* **New York: Dutton, 1957. [First published in 1782.]**

See Chapter 3, "What Is an American?" Crevecoeur

establishes the basic story of the immigrant, building America and working in self-interest.

D'Innocenzo, Michael, and Sirefman, Josef P., eds. *Immigration and Ethnicity: American Society— "Melting Pot" or "Salad Bowl"?* **Westport, CT: Greenwood Press, 1992.**

> Good background reading. The essay on "Who Were the Displaced Persons?" has a paragraph on Polish refugees.

Gordon, Milton M. *Assimilation in American Life: The Role of Race, Religion, and National Origins.* **New York: Oxford University Press, 1964.**

> Helpful as a study of immigrant group activity. Based on extensive interviewing.

Handlin, Oscar. *The Uprooted: The Epic Story of the Great Migrations That Made the American People.* **Boston: Little, Brown, 1952.**

> A classic account of immigration history, with chapters on peasant origins, the crossing, new work in the New World, religious life, and the promise the United States has held for generations of immigrants.

Hansen, Marcus Lee. *The Atlantic Migration: 1607–1860.* **Cambridge: Harvard University Press, 1940.**

> A history from the colonial period to the great migration in the early twentieth century. Illustrations and bibliography.

Higham, John. *Strangers in the Land: Patterns of American Nativism 1860–1925.* **New Brunswick, NJ: Rutgers University Press, 1955.**

> A comprehensive study of nativist (U.S.-born) responses to immigrants. Contains several passages on early attempts by the United States to discourage Polish immigrants.

Kennedy, John F. *A Nation of Immigrants*. **New York: Harper & Row, 1964.**

A succinct overview, with appendixes on the chronology of immigration and suggested reading.

Neidle, Cecyle. *The New Americans*. **New York: Twayne, 1967.**

A concise history of American immigration from the colonial period to the 1930s, with excerpts from the writings of famous travelers to the United States, immigrants, immigrant leaders, political activists and politicians, union leaders, and professional writers. Contains a bibliography.

Scott, Franklin D. *The Peopling of America: Perspectives on Immigration*. **Washington, DC: American Historical Association, 1972.**

Sections on migration history, the colonial period in North America, beginnings of the big surge (1783–1865), mass migrations of 1865–1914. Includes a bibliographical essay.

Vecoli, Rudolph J., and Sinke, Suzanne M. *A Century of European Migrations, 1830–1930*. **Urbana: University of Illinois Press, 1991.**

Part 1 has an excellent overview of migration and immigration patterns.

POLISH IMMIGRANT HISTORY

Abbott, Edith. *Immigration: Select Documents and Case Records*. **New York: Arno Press, 1969. [First published in 1924.]**

Fascinating documents relating to the transportation of immigrants in the nineteenth and twentieth centuries.

Altschuler, Glenn C. *Race, Ethnicity, and Class in American Social Thought 1865–1919*. **Arlington Heights, IL: Harlan Davidson, 1982.**

Chapter 2, "The Flame Under the Melting Pot," has several references to Polish immigrants and their adaptation to American life. Includes a bibliographical essay.

Baker, T. Lindsay. *The First Polish Americans: Silesian Settlements in Texas.* **College Station: Texas A & M University Press, 1979.**

The founding of the first Polish American communities, life on the frontier, the Civil War and Reconstruction periods, and the twentieth century. Bibliography.

Banks, Ann. *First-Person America.* **New York: Knopf, 1980.**

See Chapter 2, "Immigrant Lives," an account of Louis Kurland's journey from Poland to Cuba to Key West. *

Bernard, Richard M. *The Poles in Oklahoma.* **Norman: University of Oklahoma Press, 1980.**

Chapters on coal miners, farmers, smelters, and refugee priests. Includes a bibliographical essay.

Blejwas, Stanislaus A., and Biskupski, Mieczyslaw B., eds. *Pastor of the Poles: Polish American Essays Presented to Right Reverend Monsignor John P. Wodarski in Honor of His Fiftieth Anniversary of His Ordination.* **New Britain, CT: Central Connecticut State College, 1982.**

Essays on Poles and the Catholic Church in the United States, Polish immigration to the United States, evolution and structure of Polonia, and American reaction to the Poles.

Bodnar, John, ed. *The Ethnic Experience in Pennsylvania.* **Lewisburg: Bucknell University Press, 1973.**

In Chapter 2, "The Polish Experience in Philadelphia: The Migrant Laborers Who Did Not Come," Caroline Golab describes Poles from various regions of Poland and the reasons for their settling in Pennsylvania, and why others chose not to come.

———. *The Transplanted: A History of Immigrants in Urban America*. Bloomington: Indiana University Press, 1987.

Chapters include "The Homeland and Capitalism," "Families Enter America," "Workers, Unions, Radicals," "The Rise of an Immigrant Middle Class," "Church and Society," "Immigrants and the Promise of American Life," and "America on Immigrant Terms."

Bodnar, John; Simon, Roger; and Weber, Michael P. *Lives of Their Own: Blacks, Italians, and Poles in Pittsburgh, 1900–1960*. Urbana: University of Illinois Press, 1982.

The first chapter provides a sensitive discussion of how to handle the experiences of different ethnic and immigrant groups.

Brown, Lawrence Guy. *Immigration: Cultural Conflicts and Social Adjustments*. New York: Longmans, 1941.

See the index for specific references to Poles.

Brozek, Andrzej. *Polish Americans 1854–1939*. Warsaw: Interpress, 1985.

Appendixes feature Polish American organizations, important dates regarding American Polonia, statistics, illustrations, maps, tables, and a bibliography.

Buczek, Daniel S. *Immigrant Pastor: The Life of the Right Reverend Monsignor Lucyan Bojnowski of New Britain, Connecticut*. Waterbury, CT: Heminway Corporation, 1974.

The story of how Monsignor Bojnowski took the lead in organizing communities of poor, illiterate, and often disoriented Polish peasants.

Bukowczyk, John J. *And My Children Did Not Know Me: A History of the Polish Americans.* **Bloomington: Indiana University Press, 1987.**

A comprehensive history, beginning in rural Poland. Contains an exceptionally thorough bibliographical essay, notes, and index.

Byington, Margaret F. *Homestead: The Households of a Mill Town.* **New York: Charities Publication Committee, 1910.**

Check index under heading of Slavs for information on the working conditions and family life of Polish immigrants at the turn of the century.

Carpenter, Niles. *Immigrants and Their Children 1920.* **Washington, DC: Government Printing Office, 1927.**

See index for references to Poles.

Coleman, Marion Moore, ed. *Polish Circuit Rider: The Texas Memoirs of Adolf Bakanowski.* **Cheshire, CT: Cherry Hill Books, 1971.**

A member of the Polish gentry sent to Texas as vicar-general of the Polish churches.

Curti, Merle. *The Making of an American Community: A Case Study of Democracy in a Frontier Community.* **Stanford: Stanford University Press, 1959.**

Contains information on Polish Americans, location of settlements, occupations, economic status, religion, relations with native groups, the Civil War, politics, education, farms, and schools.

Dinnerstein, Leonard, and Reimers, David M. *Ethnic Americans: A History of Immigration and Assimilation,* **2d ed. New York: Harper & Row, 1982.**

Includes bibliographical essay, several statistical tables, and a listing of major provisions of the U.S. immigration laws and programs.

Dinnerstein, Leonard; Nichols, Roger L.; and Reimers, David M. *Natives and Strangers: Ethnic Groups and the Building of America.* **New York: Oxford University Press, 1979.**

From the Colonial period to the 1970s. Numerous references to Poles and Polish American organizations. Includes an excellent annotated bibliography.

Di Pietro, Robert J., and Ifkovic, Edward. *Ethnic Perspectives in American Literature: Selected Essays on the European Contribution.* **New York: Modern Language Association of America, 1983.**

Contains a chapter on Polish American literature.

Domanski, F., et al. *The Contribution of the Poles to the Growth of Catholicism in the United States.* **Rome: Sacrum Poloniae Millennium, 1959.**

Includes essays on the formative years of the Polish seminary in the United States, Catholic priests of Polish descent in the United States to 1957, Polish American sisterhoods and their contribution to the Catholic Church of the United States, index of names and places, and an index of parish patrons.

Ehrlich, Richard L., ed. *Immigrants in Industrial America 1850–1920.* **Charlottesville: University Press of Virginia, 1977.**

References to Poles, patterns of migration, geographic mobility, Polish life in Philadelphia and Manchester, New Hampshire, employment of Polish women, and home ownership.

Erickson, Charlotte, ed. *Emigration from Europe 1815–1914 Select Documents.* **London: Adam & Charles Black, 1976.**

Chapters on causes of emigration, the recruitment of immigrants, journey, and arrival.

Esslinger, Dean R. *Immigrants and the City: Ethnicity and Mobility in a Nineteenth-Century Midwestern Community.* **Port Washington, NY: Kennikat Press, 1975.**

References to Poles, migration patterns, occupational mobility, residence, social mobility, and voluntary associations.

Fairchild, Henry Pratt, ed. *Immigrant Backgrounds.* **New York: John Wiley & Sons, 1927.**

See Chapter 13, "The Poles."

Fine, David M. *The City, the Immigrant, and American Fiction, 1880–1920.* **Metuchen, NJ: Scarecrow Press, 1977.**

Concerns mainly Eastern European Jewish immigrants.

Fox, Paul. *The Polish National Catholic Church.* **Scranton, PA: School of Christian Living, n.d.**

Chapters on the Catholic Church's rise and growth, the causes of its break with Rome, and its essential characteristics.

Friedel, Mieczyslaw W. *This Polish Blood in America's Veins: Sketches from the life of Polish immigrants and their descendants in America, illustrating a part of American history unknown to most Americans.* **New York: Vantage Press, 1987.**

Briefly considers Polish participation in significant American events such as the Revolutionary and Civil Wars.

Fuchs, Lawrence H. *The American Kaleidoscope: Race, Ethnicity, and the Civil Culture.* **Hanover, NH: University Press of New England, 1990.**

See Part 1, Chapter 3, "Immigration from Southern and Eastern Europe."

Galazka, Jacek, and Juszczak, Albert. *Polish Heritage Travel Guide to U.S.A. and Canada.* **Cornwall Bridge, CT: Polish Heritage Publications, 1992.**

A state-by-state description of Polish communities, organizations, and historic sites, with travel directions and pictures. Several helpful appendixes.

Golab, Caroline. *Immigrant Destinations.* **Philadelphia: Temple University Press, 1977.**

Chapters include "The European Background of Polish Migration," "The Polish Experience in Philadelphia," and "The Geography of Neighborhood." Appendixes on "Pole-Searching" and parish records.

Greeley, Andrew M. *The Catholic Experience: An Interpretation of the History of American Catholicism.* **Garden City, NY: Doubleday, 1967.**

Good background reading for considering the place of Polish Americans in the Catholic Church.

Greene, Victor. *American Immigrant Leaders 1800–1910: Marginality and Identity.* **Baltimore: Johns Hopkins University Press, 1987.**

See Chapter 6, "The Poles."

————. *For God and Country: The Rise of Polish and Lithuanian Ethnic Consciousness in America 1860–1910.* **Madison: The State History Society of Wisconsin, 1975.**

Several chapters on Chicago; also, "America's Impact on Rural Aliens."

————. *A Passion for Polka: Old-Time Ethnic Music in America.* **Berkeley: University of California Press, 1992.**

Notes the growing interest of social scientists in the recreational activities of the masses and immigrant groups.

Greene's introduction discusses the role music has played in Polish assimilation to American life.

———. **"The Polish American Worker to 1930: The 'Hunky' Image in Transition."** *The Polish Review*, Vol. 21, 1976, pp. 63–78.

An important discussion about how to view early Polish immigrant workers and the extent to which they adjusted to American culture.

———. *The Slavic Community on Strike: Immigrant Labor in Pennsylvania Anthracite.* **Notre Dame: University of Notre Dame Press, 1968.**

Extensive references to Poles, their participation in labor unions and in strikes, the Polish National Catholic Church, and the Polish National Alliance.

Greer, Colin. *Divided Society: The Ethnic Experience in America.* **New York: Basic Books, 1974.**

See Part 2, "The Nature of Assimilation," and other chapters on immigrants. Appendix 3, "Who Speaks for Ethnic America?" by Barbara Mikulski.

Grzelonski, Bogdan. *Poles in the United States of America 1776–1865.* **Warsaw: Interpress, 1976.**

Chapters on Poles in the early United States, in the U.S. Army, Tadeusz Kosciuszko, Casimir Pulaski, and Polish participation in the Civil War.

Haiman, Miecislaus. *Poland and the American Revolutionary War.* **Chicago: Polish Roman Catholic Union of America, 1932.**

Includes chapters on Kosciuszko, Pulaski, and other prominent Poles in the Revolutionary army and navy, as well as Poles among the Loyalists (supporters of the British Colonial government). Also chapters on Polish writers who traveled in America during the war.

————. *Polish Past in America 1608–1865*. Chicago: Polish Museum of America, 1974.

> Chapters on the Colonial period, early American-Polish relations, the American revolution, political immigration (1783–1865), the Civil War (Poles in both the Union and Confederate armies), and statistics on Poles in the census of 1790 and from 1820 to 1870. Contains a bibliography.

Holli, Melvin G., and Jones, Peter d'A., eds. *The Ethnic Frontier: Essays in the History of Group Survival in Chicago and the Midwest*. Grand Rapids, MI: William B. Eerdmans Publishing Co., 1977.

> See " 'Becoming American': The Role of Ethnic Leaders—Swedes, Poles, Italians, Jews," by Victor Greene; "Polish Chicago: Survival Through Solidarity," by Edward R. Kantowicz.

Horgan, T. "Polish National Catholic Church." *New Catholic Encyclopedia*, vol. XI. New York: McGraw-Hill, 1967.

> This encyclopedia entry provides an explanation of the Polish National Catholic Church, organized by the Rev. Franciszek Hodur in Scranton, Pennsylvania, in 1904.

Jasso, Guillermina. *The New Chosen People: Immigrants in the United States*. New York: Russell Sage Foundation, 1990.

> Chapters on emigration and naturalization, immigrants and the U.S. economy, and immigrants of the 1980s. Contains a bibliography.

Kajencki, Francis Casimir, ed. *Poles in the 19th-Century Southwest*. El Paso: Southwest Polonia Press, 1990.

> Essays on Poles in New Mexico. Details their pioneering efforts as merchants and soldiers. Contains a bibliography.

Kantowicz, Edward R. *Corporation Sole: Cardinal Mundelein and Chicago Catholicism*. Notre Dame: University of Notre Dame Press, 1983.

A detailed biography of the life and career of the cardinal who "put the Catholic Church on the map." References to Polish Catholics and their relationship with Mundelein.

———. *Polish American Politics in Chicago 1888–1940.* Chicago: University of Chicago Press, 1975.

Covers the immigration from Poland to Chicago, Chicago politics in the Progressive Era, national politics, the rise of Chicago and the Democratic machine, and the hopes and realities of Polish American political power. Includes maps, tables, notes, and a bibliography.

Kowalik, Jan. *The Polish Press in America.* San Francisco: R & E Research Associates, 1978.

Contains definitions, a historical outline, and chapters on the contemporary press, Polish and other ethnic publications, and the role of the Polish American press in the integration process.

Kraut, Alan M. *The Huddled Masses: The Immigrant in American Society, 1880–1921.* Arlington Heights, IL: Harlan Davidson, 1982.

Several references to Polish Americans, their adoption of an urban lifestyle, and their relationship to the Roman Catholic Church. Contains a bibliography.

Kuniczak, W. S. *My Name Is Million: An Illustrated History of the Poles in America.* Garden City, NY: Doubleday, 1978.

A concise and lively history of Polish Americans from the seventeenth century to the present. Many important and rare illustrations.

Kuzniewski, Anthony J. *Faith and Fatherland: The Polish Church War in Wisconsin, 1896–1918.* Notre Dame: University of Notre Dame Press, 1980.

The struggles of Polish Americans for a place in the hierarchy of the Roman Catholic Church in the United States.

Lerski, Jerzy Jan. *A Polish Chapter in Jacksonian America: The United States and the Polish Exiles of 1831.* **Madison: University of Wisconsin Press, 1958.**

The story of Polish exiles welcomed to the United States and treated as heroes fighting for the freedom of their enslaved country.

Lieberson, Stanley. *Ethnic Patterns in American Cities.* **New York: Free Press, 1963.**

Extensive references to Poland and Polish immigrants.

———. *A Piece of the Pie: Blacks and White Immigrants Since 1880.* **Berkeley: University of California Press, 1980.**

See Chapter 4, "The New Immigrant Groups." Additional references to Polish Americans. Contains a bibliography.

Lieberson, Stanley, and Waters, Mary C. *From Many Strands: Ethnic and Racial Groups in Contemporary America.* **New York: Russell Sage Foundation, 1980.**

References to Polish ancestry and immigrants, discussion of data on income distribution, intermarriage, occupational distribution, spatial distribution, and urban distribution. Contains a bibliography.

Liebman, Lance, ed. *Ethnic Relations in America.* **Englewood Cliffs, NJ: Prentice-Hall, 1982.**

See Chapter 1, "Ethnic Groups in American History."

Linkh, Richard M. *American Catholicism and European Immigrants (1900–1924).* **Staten Island: Center for Migration Studies, 1975.**

See Chapter 3, "Catholic Attitudes Toward the 'New' Immigrant with Particular References to the Italian and Pole." Contains a bibliography.

Lopata, Helena Znaniecki. *Polish Americans: Status Competition in an Ethnic Community.* **Englewood Cliffs, NJ: Prentice-Hall, 1976.**

Discusses Polish American lifestyle, life in Poland, relationships between Poland and Polish Americans, Polish immigration to America, Polonia's relationship to the rest of American society, and patterns of change and community life in Polonia. Contains a bibliography.

Miaso, Jozef. *The History of the Education of Polish Immigrants in the United States.* **New York: Kosciuszko Foundation, 1977.**

Chapters on the first Poles in the United States, the development of Polish settlements, Polish American organizations, schools, and educational and cultural programs. Includes illustrations of important Polish American figures and institutions.

Mocha, Frank, ed. *Poles in America: Bicentennial Essays.* **Stevens Point, WI: Worzalla Publishing Co., 1978.**

Part 1: Essays on history; religion and education; scholarship, literature, and culture; organizations and scholarly institutions.

Morawska, Ewa. *For Bread with Butter: The Life-Worlds of East Central Europeans in Johnstown, Pennsylvania, 1890–1940.* **Cambridge: Cambridge University Press, 1985.**

Entries on Polish immigration, ethnic clustering, ethnic leadership, home ownership, naturalization, occupational achievement, parishes and parochial schools, and women in ethnic organizations.

———. *The Maintenance of Ethnicity: Case Study of the Polish-American Community in Greater Boston.* **San Francisco: R & E Research Associates, 1977.**

Discussion of current literature on ethnicity and the changing definitions of the term.

Morley, Charles, ed. *Portrait of America: Letters of Henry Sienkiewicz.* **New York: Columbia University Press, 1959.**

The Polish novelist and Nobel Prize winner visited the United States in 1876–1878. His letters are an invaluable document and a rarity, since not many Eastern European visitors left such accounts of travels in the United States during the nineteenth century.

Niemcewicz, Julian Ursyn. *Under Their Vine and Fig Tree: Travels through America in 1797–1799, 1805 with Some Further Account of Life in New Jersey.* **Elizabeth, NJ: Grassmann Publishing Co., 1965.**

One of the earliest and most important records of American-Polish cultural relations. Niemcewicz was a poet, playwright, pamphleteer, politician, soldier, educator, statesman, and publisher, as well as an acute and zestful traveler. Includes excerpts from Niemcewicz's American diary and his correspondence with Thomas Jefferson.

Novotny, Ann. *Strangers at the Door: Ellis Island, Castle Garden, and the Great Immigration to America.* **New York: Viking Press, 1971.**

References to Polish immigrants throughout the volume.

Olszyk, Edmund G. *The Polish Press in America.* **Milwaukee: Marquette University Press, 1940.**

Includes a historical sketch of Polish immigration, characteristics of Poles in America, Polish organizations and public influence, the makeup, organization, and circulation of the Polish press. Contains a bibliography.

Orton, Lawrence D. *Polish Detroit and the Kolasinski Affair.* **Detroit: Wayne State University Press, 1981.**

A study of the controversial priest during the 1880s and 1890s, a period of turmoil in the Polish community. He instilled remarkable devotion in peasant immigrants but was opposed by the Church hierarchy. Includes a bibliographical essay.

Pawlowska, Harriet M. *Merrily We Sing: 105 Polish Folksongs.* **Detroit: Wayne State University Press, 1983.**

An informative foreword on the folk-tale origins of songs; points out that a new urban folklore influences many of the songs. Includes notes and bibliography.

Pencak, William; Berrol, Selma; and Miller, Randall M., eds. *Immigration to New York*. Philadelphia: Balch Institute Press, 1991.

Chapters on early immigration and the early twentieth century.

Pienkos, Angela T., ed. *Ethnic Politics in Urban America: The Polish Experience in Four Cities*. Chicago: Polish American Historical Association, 1978.

Essays on Polish Americans in Buffalo, Detroit, Milwaukee, and Chicago, as well as a comparative essay by the book's editor.

Pienkos, Donald. *For Your Freedom Through Ours: Polish American Efforts on Poland's Behalf, 1863–1991*. New York: Columbia University Press, 1991.

In addition to a history of the efforts of Polish American individuals and organizations, this book contains documents on Polish American relations and concerns, a chronology of major dates in Polish American history, and a biographical listing of the leaders of the Polish American community. Contains a bibliography, subject and name index, and photographs.

———. *One Hundred Years Young: A History of the Polish Falcons of America, 1887–1987*. Boulder, CO: East European Monographs, 1987.

A fraternal insurance organization with over 30,000 members. Includes notes and bibliography.

———. *PNA: A Centennial History of the Polish National Alliance of the United States of America*. Boulder, CO: East European Monographs, 1984.

A fraternal organization of 300,000 members. Contains a chronology, notes, and a bibliography.

―――. "Politics, Religion, and Change in Polish Milwaukee, 1900–1930." *Wisconsin Magazine of History*, Vol. 61, Spring, 1978, pp. 179–209.

Traces the growth of the Polish population in Milwaukee from the turn of the century. Contains excellent illustrations, tables, and extensive notes.

Pierce, Richard L. *The Polish in America.* Chicago: Claretian Publications, 1972.

Definitions of Poles, Polonia, Polonia in the 1970s, problems of culture and identity, and the Roman Catholic Church.

Polzin, Theresita. *The Polish Americans: When and Whither.* Pulaski, WI: Franciscan Publishers, 1973.

Several chapters on early Polish immigration (1680– 1854), the Polish community in Europe and the United States, and the social, economic, and political institutions of Polish American life.

Portes, Alejandro, and Rumbaut, Ruben G. *Immigrant America: A Portrait.* Los Angeles: University of California Press, 1990.

See especially Chapter 4, "From Immigrants to Ethnics: Identity, Citizenship, and Political Participation." Extensive notes and bibliography.

Pula, James S. *Polish Americans: An Ethnic Community.* New York: Twayne, 1995.

A detailed, comprehensive history of Polonia, or Polish America, from the 1800s to the present. Pula discusses problems faced by Polish Americans throughout history and examines the community's cohesiveness and process of assimilation.

Renkiewicz, Frank. *For God, Country, and Polonia: One Hundred Years of the Orchard Lake Schools.* Orchard Lake, MI: Center for Polish Studies and Culture, 1985.

A history of one of the more important Polish school systems. Contains bibliographical notes, chapter notes, and a chronicle of important events.

——, ed. *The Poles in America 1608–1972: A Chronology and Fact Book.* Dobbs Ferry, NY: Oceana Publications, 1973.

A detailed chronology of significant dates in Polish American history, a selection of important documents, appendixes on Polish American population by states, Polish American publications, cultural institutions, a brief bibliography of books in English, and a name index.

——, ed. *The Polish Presence in Canada and America.* Toronto: Multicultural History Society of Ontario, 1982.

Essays on immigrants in industrial society; new and old communities in villages, rural areas, and cities; religion and culture; family; the postimmigrant generation; ethnicity in postindustrial society (1940–1980); prospects for the future.

Roucek, Joseph S., and Eisenberg, Bernard, eds. *America's Ethnic Politics.* Westport, CT: Greenwood Press, 1982.

See Chapter 14, "Polish-American Ethnicity in the Political Life of the United States."

Sandberg, Neil. *Ethnic Identity and Assimilation: The Polish American Community: Case Study of Metropolitan Los Angeles.* New York: Praeger, 1974.

Chapters on definitions of ethnicity and the migration from Poland to the United States.

Santoli, Al. *New Americans: An Oral History: Immigrants and Refugees in the U.S. Today.* **New York: Viking, 1988.**

Chapter on Solidarity.

Seller, Maxine. *Ethnic Theatre in the United States.* **Westport, CT: Greenwood Press, 1983.**

Chapter 15 discusses Polish American theater.

————. *To Seek America: A History of Ethnic Life in the United States.* **New York: Jerome S. Ozer, 1977.**

Chapter 7 contains references to Polish Americans. Includes a bibliography.

Serafino, Frank. *West of Warsaw.* **Hamtramck, MI: Avenue Publishing Co., 1983.**

The story of a Polish enclave within the borders of Detroit, its roots in Poland, its early immigrant population, its changing character through two wars, the decline of the auto industry, and its future prospects. Includes notes and bibliography.

Shenton, James P., and Brown, Gene. *Ethnic Groups in American Life.* **New York: Arno Press, 1978.**

Several references to Polish immigrants, Polish American men as workers, husbands, and fathers, Polish Americans in Detroit and Hamtramck, Michigan, and Polish Jewish immigrants. Contains a bibliography.

Simor, George. *Guide to the Archives of the Polish Institute of Arts and Sciences of America.* **New York: Polish Institute of Arts and Sciences of America, 1988.**

An indispensable resource for research into Polish American history, the role of immigrants, and the impact of emigration from Poland. Includes documentation on prominent Polish American scholars, artists, and writers, oral histories, literary and theatrical criticism, records of statements by Polish statesmen and leaders, original documents dating back to the fourteenth and fifteenth centuries, and an extensive collection of periodicals and newspapers.

Skendzel, Eduard Adam. *The Kolasinski Story: Priest-Protector of Detroit's Pioneer Polish Immigrants or Father of Polish American Church Independentism.* **Grand Rapids, MI: Littleshield Press, 1979.**

> A sympathetic biography of a "grass-roots" priest battling against the Church hierarchy, it also reveals the lives of Detroit's earliest Polish immigrants.

Sowell, Thomas, ed. *Essays and Data on American Ethnic Groups.* **New York: Urban Institute, 1978.**

> See Chapter 3 on European immigrant groups. Includes several tables on Polish Americans, showing personal income distribution by sex, family income distribution, and occupational and educational distribution by sex. Other references to Polish Americans.

Spear, Allan H. *Black Chicago: The Making of a Negro Ghetto 1890–1920.* **Chicago: University of Chicago Press, 1967.**

> Numerous references to Polish immigrants.

Steiner, Edward A. *The Immigrant Tide: Its Ebb and Flow.* **New York: Fleming H. Revell Co., 1909.**

> See Chapters 14 and 15 on Slavs; specific references to Poland and Polish Americans.

Stephenson, George M. *A History of American Immigration 1820–1924.* **New York: Ginn and Co., 1926.**

> See Chapter 9, "The Slavs."

Taylor, Philip. *The Distant Magnet: European Emigration to the U.S.A.* **New York: Harper & Row, 1971.**

See Chapters 9 and 10, "Immigrant Workers and American Environments," and "Immigrant Communities," for comments on Polish Americans and the Catholic Church and other institutions. Contains a bibliography.

Thernstrom, Stephan, ed. *Harvard Encyclopedia of American Ethnic Groups*. Cambridge: Harvard University Press, 1980.

Thematic essays on assimilation and pluralism, concepts of ethnicity, education, family patterns, immigration, literature and ethnicity, religious resources and research centers, and survey research. Individual entries on ethnic groups, including Poles. Includes maps, tables, and a bibliography.

Thomas, William I., and Znaniecki, Florian. *The Polish Peasant in Europe and America*. Urbana: University of Illinois Press, 1984.

A comprehensive history including fascinating letters written by Polish immigrants.

Van Norman, Louis E. *Poland: The Knight Among Nations*. New York: Fleming H. Revell Co., 1907.

See the last chapter on Poles in the United States.

Weed, Perry L. *The White Ethnic Movement and Ethnic Politics*. New York: Praeger, 1973.

See Chapter 5, "Detroit's Black Polish Conference"; Chapter 6, "The Emergence of Ethnic Politics in the 1960s"; and Chapter 8 on the Republicans' ethnic appeals to Poles. Contains a bibliography.

Weyl, Walter E. "Jan, the Polish Miner." *The Outlook*, Vol. 94, March 26, 1910, pp. 709–717.

A sympathetic story of an immigrant's exposure to American culture and politics; also a fascinating account of American attitudes toward immigrants.

Wiedzerzak, Joseph W. *A Polish Chapter in Civil War America: The Effects of the January Insurrection on American Opinion and Diplomacy.* **New York: Twayne, 1967.**

> The impact of Poles who came to the United States after the Polish insurrection of 1861, which challenged Russian rule of Poland.

Wlodarski, Stephen. *The Origins and Growth of the Polish National Catholic Church.* **Scranton, PA: Polish National Catholic Church, 1974.**

> Chapters on immigration of Poles to the United States, religious and Church life of Polonia, the origins of the PNCC (1897–1907), its growth (1908–1972), and its ideology. Contains a bibliography.

Wood, Arthur Evans. *Hamtramck: A Sociological Study of a Polish American Community.* **New Haven: College and University Press, 1955.**

> Chapters on Hamtramck and its setting in the Detroit area, its politics (1900–1942), the school system, delinquency and crime, cultural organizations and leisure, and patterns of family life.

Wrobel, Paul. *Our Way: Family, Parish and Neighborhood in a Polish American Community.* **Notre Dame: University of Notre Dame Press, 1979.**

> Concentrates on working-class Polish Americans in a Detroit neighborhood in the early 1970s.

Wytrwal, Joseph A. *America's Polish Heritage: A Social History of the Poles in America.* **Detroit: Endurance Press, 1961.**

> Begins with the first Polish immigrants in 1608. Discusses causes of emigration, the activities of several Polish American organizations, the Polish American during World War II, and Polish American cultural relationships. Contains a bibliography.

Zeitlin, Richard H. "White Eagles in the North Woods: Polish Immigration to Rural Wisconsin." *The Polish Review,* **Vol. 25, 1980, pp. 69–92.**

Contains fascinating information not only about Poles who settled in rural areas, but also about the dynamics of Polish emigration from 1865 to 1920.

Zunz, Olivier. *The Changing Face of Inequality: Urbanization, Industrial Development, and Immigrants in Detroit, 1880–1920.* **Chicago: University of Chicago Press, 1982.**

Extensive references to Polish Americans: age distribution, community conflict, education, family economy, family size, family structure, fertility, home building and ownership, household organization, language, marriage patterns, politics, residential concentration, schools, and social mobility. Illustrated.

Zurawski, Joseph W. *Polish American History and Culture: A Classified Bibliography.* **Chicago: Polish Museum of America, 1975.**

Chapters on Polish history and culture; Polish American history; the geographical distribution of Polish Americans; Polish American social accounts, religious accounts, cultural accounts, educational accounts, economic accounts, and national policy accounts; U.S. foreign policy and Poland; Polish American biographical accounts; Polish Americans in U.S. novels, short stories, poetry, and theater.

POLISH AMERICAN AUTOBIOGRAPHIES

Hoffman, Eva. *Lost in Translation.* **New York: E.P. Dutton, 1989.**

A beautiful evocation of her experience as a Jewish woman in Poland and in the United States.

Milosz, Czeslaw. "Biblical Heirs and Modern Evils: A Polish Poet in California." In *The Immigrant Experience: The Anguish of Becoming American.* Edited by Thomas C. Wheeler. New York: Dial Press, 1971.

> Milosz describes his adjustment to a new life in the United States.

———. *Native Realm: A Search for Self-Definition.* New York: Doubleday, 1968.

> Republished in paperback by University of California Press in 1981. A Nobel Prize winner, Milosz describes his life from childhood to the early 1950s.

———. *The Year of the Hunter.* New York: Farrar, Straus & Giroux, 1994.

> A diary covering the period August 1987 to August 1988, which also ranges widely over the author's life both in the United States and Poland. Includes a biographical glossary and notes.

Morrison, Joan, and Zabusky, Charlotte Fox. *American Mosaic: The Immigrant Experience in the Words of Those Who Lived It.* Pittsburgh: University of Pittsburgh Press, 1993.

> See statements by Sophie Zurowski (p. 53), Casimir Kopek (p. 61), Zosia Kaminsky (p.68), Tanja Shimiewsky (p. 154), Wojtek Pobog (p. 161), Joseph Bergman (p. 242), and Felix Kucynski (p. 255).

Namias, June. *First Generation: In the Words of Twentieth-Century American Immigrants.* Boston: Beacon Press, 1978.

> See " 'Moshe Lodsky'—From Russian Poland to the Lower East Side."

Seller, Maxine Schwartz, ed. *Immigrant Women.* Philadelphia: Temple University Press, 1981.

See Part 1, Chapter 2, "My Education and Aspirations Demanded More," by Marie Zakrezewska; Part 3, Chapter 2, "A Physician in the 'First True Woman's Hospital' in the World," by Marie Zakrezewska; Part 5, Chapter 2, "'Let Us Join Hands': The Polish Women's Alliance," by Thaddeus Radzialowski; Part 6, Chapter 1, "For Nickels and Dimes: 'A Book Was a . . . Precious Thing'" by Monica Krawczyk; Chapter 2, "The Lessons Which Most Influenced My Life . . . Came from My Parents," by Harriet Pawlowska; Part 8, Chapter 6, "We Can Begin to Move Toward Sisterhood," by Barbara Mikulski.

Chapter 2
Poland, Polish Americans, and the History of Immigration

Poland is situated in the heart of Europe, bordering on Germany in the west, on the Baltic Sea and Russia in the north, on Lithuania, Belarus, and Ukraine (all part of the former Soviet Union) in the east, and on the Czech Republic and Slovakia in the south. Its geographical position has contributed both to its periods of power and weakness. Poles as a separate, Slavic group asserted themselves in the tenth century. Led by Duke Miesko I (960–992) of the Piast dynasty, Poles gradually converted to Christianity. Throughout the Middle Ages, Polish power waxed and waned as the Piasts expanded and defended their domain against German emperors and the rulers of Hungary, Bohemia, Pomerania, Denmark, and Russia. The Piast line culminated in Casimir III (1310–1370), a brilliant administrator and political leader, who established a tolerant, enlightened society that welcomed other peoples, including the Jews.

After Casimir III's death, title to the Polish kingdom passed to his nephew, Louis I of Hungary, and then to his daughter Jadwiga, who married Ladislaus Jagiello, grand duke of Lithuania. Ladislaus founded the Jagiello dynasty, which ruled Poland until 1572. This period, especially the sixteenth century, is considered the country's golden age. Poland championed the cause of defending Europe against Muslim invasions; it defeated the Teutonic knights, and its economy and culture prospered. Poles honor the astronomer Copernicus (1473–1543) as one of their great contributors to modern science.

Tadeusz Kosciuszko was a hero in both the Polish and American struggles for independence.

Even as Poland regarded itself as holding together the heart of Europe, internal dissension developed between the Jagiellos and the Polish aristocracy, growing in power and keen to assert its rights through legislative government. The *liberum veto* allowed any member of the Sejm (the Polish parliament) to dissolve it or even to annul previous decisions, claiming that all actions must be unanimous if they were to be accepted as good for the whole country. Polish kings found it difficult to pursue consistent policies as factions developed among the aristocracy. No other group could help to overcome this fractious situation, since the middle class was largely Jewish and German, and the lower class (the serfs) had virtually no rights. A kind of democracy prevailed only among the aristocrats, but this egalitarianism for the upper class only made their rivalries fiercer.

Polish attempts to conquer Russia failed, and Charles X of Sweden successfully invaded Poland in 1655 while Russia attacked from the east. Poles did manage to regroup and save part of their country, but by the end of the seventeenth century it had been so severely weakened that it could not withstand plundering raids by its neighbors.

From 1795 to 1918 Poland ceased to exist as a country, but Poles maintained their identity by remaining fiercely loyal to the Catholic Church and by perpetuating the stories of Polish nationhood in the work of great poets such as Adam Mickiewicz (1798–1855).

Because Poland was dominated by foreign powers, and many Poles lost their livelihoods and sometimes their lives rebelling against Russian or Prussian authority, Poles looked to other countries for inspiration and for refuge. The great Polish patriots Casimir Pulaski (1748–1799) and Tadeusz Kosciuszko (1746–1817) fought with distinction in the American Revolution. Towns and streets have been named after these heroes; some public parks feature stirring statues dedicated to their sacrifices for freedom in the United States.

Poles in the hundreds of thousands came to the United States in the great wave of immigration that lasted from 1901 to 1910. Like most immigrants, they were attracted to

Polish-born Kazimierz Rutowski and his daughter Halina peruse a booklet on American citizenship after he took the oath of citizenship in Paramus, New Jersey.

the American ideal of life, liberty, and the pursuit of happiness. Most Polish immigrants were peasants with little formal education; yet they adapted quickly to working in Pittsburgh's steel mills, in Detroit's automobile factories, in Chicago's stockyards, and in other urban areas. They followed other immigrant groups in joining labor unions and participating in local politics. Often the first generation of Polish immigrants did not learn English. Instead they spoke a mixture of English and Polish words that was ungrammatical but useful for jobs that required strong muscles and discipline, rather than language skills and writing ability. Polish immigrants were part of huge public works projects such as the building of the Detroit-Windsor tunnel in 1930. They worked hard and sent their children to public schools.

Many Polish women and girls who had not worked outside the home in Poland were forced to do so in the United States out of economic necessity. They earned extra money for their families by working as unskilled workers, domestic helpers, factory workers, seamstresses, or in other service fields. Sometimes a household would increase its income by taking in boarders, in which case the woman of the household was responsible for cooking, cleaning, and washing clothes not only for her own family, but for the guests as well.

The second generation of Polish Americans, born in the United States, were usually bilingual and helped their parents adjust to the rapid changes of twentieth-century American society. The second generation joined their parents in honoring the traditions and customs of "the old country." Often they would join a "Dom Polski," a "Polish Home" that featured events celebrating their Polish heritage. The third generation learned dances from their grandparents' native land and dressed up in old-country costumes. There was some Polish language instruction, but usually the third generation did not speak Polish, though it might be familiar with basic vocabulary having grown up hearing parents speak the language.

The overwhelming majority of Polish immigrants to the United States were already here when Poland regained its

The combination of Polish Americans' belief in American anti-Communist values and their fierce loyalty to an independent Poland led to an outcry against the Soviet domination of Poland. Polish Americans express their anger in this 1948 "Loyalty Parade."

independence in 1918 at the end of World War I. Many Polish Americans visited the old country, sent money to relatives, and maintained fond ties with Poland. But very few returned home permanently. Indeed, the United States was now their home, and they were proud of it. Poles rose to prominence in the United States, becoming labor union leaders, politicians, and business executives. Poles strongly supported the Catholic Church and saw it as part of their American identity as well. In the early 1900s, the Polish National Catholic Church was organized by a priest in Scranton, Pennsylvania.

Polish Americans felt even more patriotic and loyal to their new country when Poland's brief period of independence ended in 1939, when Germany and the Soviet Union started World War II by invading Poland. Great Britain and France declared war on Germany, vowing to defend their Polish ally. When Germany invaded the Soviet Union in

Author Jerzy Kosinski is an example of a Polish Jew who made his home in the United States.

1941, the latter became an ally of the United States and Great Britain, and Poles supported the war effort; however, they worried that the Soviet Union would dominate Poland and much of Eastern Europe. The Polish army under Marshal Józef Klemens Pilsudski had defeated the Red Army in 1920, but Poles realized that a Soviet victory over Germany in World War II made Poland extremely vulnerable. (See *The Face of War*, listed in the **Resources** section, for Martha Gellhorn's reports on Polish distrust of Soviet intentions.) That is exactly what happened: Poland became a Soviet satellite, and Polish Americans bitterly opposed the spread of communism in the 1940s and 1950s in Central and Eastern Europe.

Polish Americans viewed their native land as a battleground of history, while they saw the United States as a land of redemption, where Polish sacrifices for freedom were acknowledged and rewarded. The United States was staunchly anti-Communist. It believed in the rights of the individual. It provided equality of opportunity. These were values that Poles had not been able to practice in Europe.

Polish Jews

Poland has always been a predominantly Catholic country, but until the end of World War II it had a rich multiethnic population, including Germans, Lithuanians, and especially Jews. One out of ten Poles was a Jew. Jews had thrived in Poland; they had also been persecuted. Poles have pointed to their long tradition of tolerance and insisted that their honorable treatment of minorities compares favorably to the record of other European countries. Yet many Jewish families have encountered Polish anti-Semitism. Claude Lanzmann's great movie on the Holocaust, *Shoah*, consisting of interviews with concentration camp survivors, German guards, and Polish peasants who lived in the vicinity of the camps, portrays instances where Polish attitudes seemed to sanction the Nazi atrocities. On the other hand, there are numerous examples of Poles risking their own lives to protect and conceal Jews from Nazis rounding up victims for death camps. You will find a record of both kinds of

Polish responses in the **Resources** section, which also describes several books on the Warsaw Ghetto, the enclave of Jews systematically persecuted by the Nazis. Eventually the Warsaw Ghetto Jews rebelled against the enormous power of the Nazis; although the Ghetto was annihilated, it remains an enduring symbol of both human suffering and courage.

Polish Jews often have mixed feelings about Poland. They may not consider themselves Polish as such, but this does not mean that Poland has not shaped their identity, nor that they do not treasure aspects of their Polish past. But Jews, except for those willing to assimilate, lived quite apart from their fellow Poles in pre-World War II Poland. Several readings on Polish Jews in the **Resources** section of this chapter explore the lives of Polish Jews before and after the Holocaust. The **Resources** section in Chapter 3 also describes several books for those interested in tracing their Jewish roots in Poland.

Contemporary Poland

Since 1980, American perceptions of Poland have changed greatly. First was the growth of the independent labor union, Solidarity, led by the charismatic Lech Walesa, an electrician who spoke in earthy yet devout language and challenged the Communist status quo. Polish workers and intellectuals united to oppose the Soviet-backed government. Although Solidarity was eventually outlawed, and the Polish military government, headed by General Wojciech Jaruzelski, imposed martial law—taking away the few individual rights people had and imposing strict censorship on all communications media—it is evident now that Poland in the early 1980s was heralding the end of Communist domination in Eastern Europe.

Soon new refugees from Poland arrived in the United States. These were not Polish farmers or peasants but university professors and other professionals. They were granted political asylum. Many of them, like Stanislav Baranczyk (Professor of Polish Language and Literature at Harvard University), began writing for American publications.

Marie Curie, seen here at work in her Paris laboratory, is famous for discovering the elements radium and polonium, the latter named for her native Poland.

Poland's history became of international concern, and its Solidarity movement inspired dissenters throughout Central and Eastern Europe—as well as many Polish Americans who traveled to Poland.

With the tearing down of the Berlin Wall in November 1989 and the demise of the Soviet Union in December 1991, Polish Americans and Polish immigrants are entering a new phase. Now Poland, which has abandoned its centrally planned Communist economy, is emulating the United States's capitalistic example, although many ex-Communists are part of the country's new government and the form of the economy is still evolving. Poland, for all its problems of adjustment to a new political and economic system, is one of the prospering nations in the new Eastern Europe, with a vibrant political culture expressing a great diversity of opinion.

Polish Greatness

Poland's tragic and sublime history has produced such great scientists and artists as Marie Sklodowska-Curie (1859–1906), who discovered radium, and the composer Frederic Chopin (1810–1849). One of Poland's native sons, Jozef Konrad Korzeniowski (1857–1924), emigrated to England and became one of the masters of English prose, changing his name to Joseph Conrad. A more recent immigrant to the post-World War II United States, Jerzy Kosinski (1993–1991), won several prestigious awards for his novels and made contemporary American culture the subject of his writing. Polish immigrant Zbigniew Brzezinski (1928–) was President Carter's national security adviser at the same time Poland's Cardinal Wojtyla was elected Pope John Paul II. In fact, in 1980, Poles in Poland used to joke that they had their man in Washington and their man in Rome—now all they needed was their man in Moscow. Indeed, Pope John Paul II's first visit to his native land in 1978 is credited with spurring people to take actions that eventually doomed the Communist government in Poland.

Today more than 15 million people of Polish descent are

living in the United States and nearly 400,000 in Canada. Chicago has close to 1 million Polish Americans. Hamtramck, a city surrounded by the Detroit metropolitan area, is one of many Polish enclaves in America where you can hear Polish spoken every day in shops, on the streets, and in homes. The Polish National Alliance has more than 325,000 members, and there are thousands of Polish Americans in organizations such as the Polish Catholic Union, the Polish-American Congress, the Polish Women's Alliance, the Polish Falcons, and the American Council of Polish Cultural Clubs. Poles and their descendants have distinguished themselves in all walks of life. Think of the baseball great Carl Yaztrzemski of the Boston Red Sox, movie actress Loretta Swit, symphony conductor Leopold Stokowski, former senator and vice-presidential candidate Edmund Muskie, and a legend in the cosmetics industry, Helena Rubinstein.

The successes of Polish Americans are not surprising; they should be measured against the impressive contributions Poles have made to European culture. As artists, soldiers, statesmen—people in all walks of life—Poles have made extraordinary contributions, strengthening the traditions of Western civilization and helping to define the promise and achievement of a new land and a new identity.

Resources

HISTORY OF POLAND

Benes, Vaclav, and Pounds, Norman J. G. *Poland*. New York: Praeger, 1970.

A history that argues vigorously for the importance of an independent Polish state. See especially Part 3, "The Political Background of Modern Poland," and Part 4, "Poland a Soviet Satellite." Includes an appendix of place names (giving spellings in English, French, German, and Russian) and a bibliography.

Davies, Norman. *God's Playground: A History of Poland*. New York: Columbia University Press, 1984.

This two-volume study is the most up-to-date, reliable, and readable history in English.

————. *Heart of Europe: A Short History of Poland*. Oxford: Oxford University Press, 1984.

Works backward from the events in the early 1980s to eighteenth-century Poland, emphasizing those factors that were most important in shaping the country's present. Includes maps, genealogical tables, and a gazetteer.

Dziewanowski, M. K. *The Communist Party of Poland: An Outline of History*. Cambridge: Harvard University Press, 1959.

Chapters on the beginning of socialism in Poland (1832–1892); the revolutions in Poland and Russia (1904–1905) and their aftermath; the history of the Communist Party in Poland during World War I; its status in the interwar period; the seizure and consolidation of power after World War II; purges and mergers with other parties in the 1950s; the party's relationship with peasants; the Church; and efforts to reform the party. Contains a bibliography.

Gellhorn, Martha. *The Face of War*. New York: Atlantic Monthly Press, 1988.

Two chapters of interviews with Poles during World War II: "Three Poles" and "The Carpathian Lancers."

———. *The View from the Ground*. New York: Atlantic Monthly Press, 1988.

The chapter "Return to Poland" describes interviews with Poles during the 1960s.

Giergielewicz, Mieczyslaw, ed. *Polish Civilization: Essays and Studies*. New York: New York University Press, 1979.

Essays on Polish peasant rituals, towns in medieval Poland, the Polish Reformation, the protection of Jewish rights, Polish Catholicism, the working class in Poland, and the concentration camps.

Gieysztor, Aleksander, et al. *History of Poland*. Warsaw: Polish Scientific Publishers, 1968.

From medieval Poland to 1939, with a conclusion covering the first years of Communist rule after World War II. Written from the perspective of the ruling Communist Party. Includes maps, chronological tables, and bibliography.

Gross, Jan Tomasz. *Polish Society Under German Occupation: The Generalgouvernement 1939–1944*. Princeton: Princeton University Press, 1979.

The German occupation of Poland lasted longer than that of any other country in World War II. It was also the harshest, given the Germans' racial views and the imposition of concentration camps. Gross studies the impact on

Polish society of this prolonged disaster. Should be read in conjunction with Jerzy Kosinski's novel *The Painted Bird.*

Halecki, O. *A History of Poland.* New York: Roy, 1976.

The ninth edition of a classic work describing Poland's origins to the mid-1950s. Includes several maps.

Karski, Jan. *The Great Powers and Poland 1919–1945: From Versailles to Yalta.* New York: University Press of America, 1985.

Chapters on the question of Polish independence during World War I; the attitudes of Czarist Russia, the Western allies, and of Poles in the West; the Versailles peace conference; the Polish-Bolshevik War; Pilsudski's rule in Poland during the interwar period; Franco-Polish relations; the era of appeasement (1937–1938) and Poland's role in it; Poland during World War II; the Warsaw uprising; Yalta and the postwar agreements that decided Poland's fate. Contains a bibliography.

———. *Story of a Secret State.* Boston: Houghton Mifflin, 1944.

Karski's dramatic experiences during the war, his imprisonment in Russia, his escape, experiences in devastated Poland, and later missions during the war, and his undercover work and experience in the Warsaw ghetto.

Kolankiewicz, George, and Lewis, Paul G. *Poland: Politics, Economics, and Society.* New York: Pinter Publishers, 1988.

Chapters on Poland's history and traditions, social structure and social welfare, structures of political rule, economy, economic and political policy, and contemporary history. Includes bibliography, map of provincial boundaries and capitals, figures showing the structure of national and political government, and numerous tables.

Lednicki, Waclaw. *Russia, Poland, and the West.* New York: Roy, 1953.

Chapters on Russia, its writers, and the West, the relationship between Polish and Russian writers, Dostoevsky, and Poland.

Lukas, Richard C. *The Forgotten Holocaust: The Poles Under German Occupation 1939–1944.* Lexington: University Press of Kentucky, 1986.

Chapters on the Polish Underground, the relationship between Poles and Jews, the Polish government, the Home Army, the Jews, and the Warsaw uprising. Contains a bibliography and maps.

Lukas, Richard, ed. *Out of the Inferno: Poles Remember the Holocaust.* Lexington: University Press of Kentucky, 1989.

Autobiographies derived from depositions and interviews—all first-hand accounts that have not been published before.

McLean, Moore W. *Notable Personages of Polish Ancestry.* Detroit: Unique Press, 1938.

A biographical dictionary with separate sections on artists and architects; composers, musicians, and dramatic artists; military and naval leaders; professors and educators; religious figures; scientists; statesmen and rulers. Includes a selected bibliography of books on Poland.

Narkiewicz, Olga A. *The Green Flag: Polish Populist Politics 1867–1970.* Totowa, NJ: Rowman and Littlefield, 1976.

One of the few studies of its kind in English. Chapters on the peasants and their organizations, electoral reform, political intrigue, land reform, populism and Pilsudski, peasant parties and socialism. Contains a bibliography and glossary.

Novak, Jan. *Courier from Warsaw.* Detroit: Wayne State University Press, 1982.

An eyewitness to the Polish drama of World War II. A riveting account of Novak's secret trips to Scandinavia, Britain, North Africa, Switzerland, and France, barely eluding the Gestapo. Includes illustrations, photographs, maps. Foreword by Zbigniew Brzezinski.

Olszer, Krystyna, ed. *For Your Freedom and Ours: Polish Progressive Spirit from the 14th Century to the Present*. New York: Frederick Ungar, 1981.

Ends with the Gdansk agreements forged between the Solidarity movement and the Communist government in 1980. Essentially a compilation of historic documents by Poland's poets, philosophers, statesmen, other intellectuals, and workers.

Pfeiffer, Christine. *Poland: Land of Freedom Fighters*. Minneapolis, MN: Dillon Press, 1984.

Clear, concise history of Poland, including a "fast facts" section, maps, photographs, a listing of Polish consulates in the United States and Canada, list of Polish phrases, adjectives, and titles with a pronunciation guide, glossary, bibliography, and index.

Pogonowski, Cyprian. *Poland: A Historical Atlas*. New York: Hippocrene Books, 1987.

Maps of Poland show its place in Western civilization (966–1986), its hereditary monarchy (840–1370), its transition to constitutional monarchy (1493–1569), the Polish republics from 1569 to the present. Also contains a detailed chronology of Poland's constitutional and political development, notes on its indigenous democratic process and on the evolution of Polish identity, plus appendixes on coats of arms of Polish towns.

***Polish Encyclopedia*, 3 vols. New York: Arno Press, 1972. [First published 1926.]**

Volume 1: History of literature; separate chapters on the Renaissance, the Baroque, Pseudo-Classicism,

Romanticism, and Contemporary Literature. Two chapters on Polish history to 1914. Volume 2: Territory and population, geography, ethnography, history of the population of independent Poland, Poland in the sixteenth to nineteenth centuries, marriages, births, mortality, natural increase, population according to sex and age, Prussian Poland, Austrian Poland, the kingdom of Poland, Jews in Poland, the population of present-day Poland. Volume 3: Economic life of Poland, natural wealth, Prussian Poland, Galicia and Silesia, kingdom of Poland, Lithuania and Ruthenia. Includes maps and bibliography.

Polonsky, Antony, and Drukier, Boleslaw. *The Beginnings of Communist Rule in Poland.* **London: Routledge & Kegan Paul, 1980.**

Helpful maps, glossary of political terms, short political biographies of the principals in postwar Polish history, key documents from this period, and several photographs of the World War II period.

Sharp, Samuel L. *Poland: White Eagle on a Red Field.* **Cambridge: Harvard University Press, 1953.**

Not a full-fledged history, but an account of those factors that have shaped contemporary Poland. Separate chapters devoted to the period between the two world wars, World War II, the Communist government, American-Polish relations, and the future of Poland. Includes maps of Poland's partitions and territorial changes.

Stasiewski, B. "Poland." *New Catholic Encyclopedia,* **vol. XI. New York: McGraw-Hill, 1967.**

Maps, statistical tables, illustrations, and bibliography.

Steven, Stewart. *The Poles.* **New York: Macmillan, 1982.**

A short history by a political and diplomatic journalist who has traveled widely in Poland and is married to a Polish woman. A popular, rather than scholarly work, it benefits from Steven's extensive interviews with Poles during the first days of the Solidarity movement. Includes notes and bibliography.

Szczepanski, Jan. *Polish Society.* **New York: Random House, 1970.**

Explores social change in Poland from the interwar period to the late 1960s. Traditional Polish values and the new Communist order are studied for their impact on each other. Includes notes and bibliography.

Tazbir, Janusz. *A State Without Stakes: Polish Religious Toleration in the Sixteenth and Seventeenth Centuries.* **New York: Kosciuszko Foundation, 1973.**

Poland's role during the Reformation, its tolerance of religious dissidents, the climate of religious coexistence, the development of toleration, and how this unusual era ended in the eighteenth century.

Topolski, Jerzy. *An Outline History of Poland.* **Warsaw: Interpress Publishers, 1986.**

Begins with a description of Polish territory in the sixth century and ends in 1980. Told from the point of view of Polish Communist authorities. Includes photographs, genealogical tables, a bibliography in Polish, maps, and index.

Toranska, Teresa. *"Them": Stalin's Polish Puppets.* **New York: Harper & Row, 1987.**

A sharply critical portrait of the Soviet-dominated rulers of post-World War II Poland. Toranska was a Polish journalist who brought to light much inside information on the government. Her book was circulated underground, and she moved to France in 1985. Includes an index of proper names.

Van Norman, Louis E. *Poland: The Knight Among Nations.* **New York: Fleming H. Revell Co., 1907.**

Chapters on Poland's role in history, Cracow, the domination of Poland by Germany, Russia, and Austria, the Polish peasant, Polish music, Polish country life and customs, and Poles in the United States.

Wandycz, Piotr S. *The Lands of Partitioned Poland, 1795–1918*. Seattle: University of Washington Press, 1974.

Chapters on the aftermath of the partitions, the age of insurrections, and the road to independence. Contains a bibliographical essay.

Watt, Richard M. *Bitter Glory: Poland and Its Fate 1918 to 1939*. New York: Simon & Schuster, 1979.

Begins with a chapter on Poland's great interwar leader Pilsudski, his record of governing, the country's political and economic life, and its "fourth partition," the simultaneous German and Soviet invasions in September 1939. Includes notes, maps, and bibliography.

Zaloga, Steven, and Madej, Victor. *The Polish Campaign 1939*. New York: Hippocrene Books, 1985.

The history of the Polish army 1918–1939, its organization and strategic plans, equipment, the September 1939 campaign, a combat chronology of the Polish units in the 1939 war, and appendixes on the German and Red Army order of battle. Contains a bibliography.

Zamoyski, Adam. *The Polish Way: A Thousand-Year History of the Poles and Their Culture*. New York: Franklin Watts, 1988.

A vivid account of Polish history, featuring illustrations, figures, and maps, a genealogy of Polish kings, a selection of Polish coats of arms, portraits of Polish rulers and writers, and color pictures of Polish art. Concentrates on Poland in its European context. Includes bibliography.

Zawodny, J. K. *Death in the Forest: The Story of the Katyn Forest Massacre*. Notre Dame: University of Notre Dame Press, 1962.

More than 15,000 Polish soldiers, including 800 doctors, were murdered at Katyn in 1941. For years the Soviet Union denied responsibility and accused the Germans of the massacre, but evidence clearly pointed to the former— as Zawodny's book demonstrates. Recently the Soviet Union has accepted the evidence convicting it of the crime. Zawodny not only investigates the massacre but shows how postwar relations between Poland and the Soviet Union were darkened by this atrocity.

POLISH JEWS AND THE WARSAW GHETTO

Aaron, Frieda W. *Bearing the Unbearable: Yiddish and Polish Poetry in the Ghettos and Concentration Camps*. **Albany: State University of New York Press, 1990.**

Divided into sections: "Poetry as Documentation," "Morale, Moral Resistance, and the Crisis of Faith," "Issues of Resistance." Includes extensive quotations from poetry, notes, and bibliography.

Ainsztein, Reuben. *The Warsaw Ghetto Revolt*. **New York: Holocaust Library, 1979.**

Chapters on the Jewish plans for resistance, the uprising and its aftermath. Contains notes and bibliography.

Bartoszewski, Wladyslaw. *The Warsaw Ghetto: A Christian's Testimony*. **Boston: Beacon Press, 1987.**

An important foreword by Polish writer Stanislaw Lem detailing Bartoszewski's efforts to rescue Jews from destruction.

Checinski, Michel. *Poland: Communism, Nationalism, Anti-Semitism*. **New York: Karz-Cohl Publishing, 1982.**

Based on more than eighty interviews the author conducted with Communist party high officials, former security and military officers, leaders of Jewish cultural and

economic institutions in Poland, and former Polish jour-
nalists. Chapters on the Jewish Communists after World
War II, the rise of a police state, the relaxation of Communist power in 1956, and then the reimposition of Soviet-
style anti-Semitism.

Cowan, Neil M., and Cowan, Ruth Schwartz. *Our
Parents' Lives: The Americanization of Eastern
European Jews.* **New York: Basic Books, 1989.**

Several references to Poland.

Dobroszycki, Lucjan, ed. *The Chronicle of the Lodz
Ghetto 1941–1944.* **New Haven: Yale University Press,
1984.**

Chronicle kept in the archive of the Jewish Administration
of the Lodz ghetto, an enclave of Polish Jews facing annihilation by the Nazis. Provides a horrifying look at the
daily destruction of lives in the Holocaust.

Dubnow, S. M. *History of the Jews in Russia and
Poland from the Earliest Times Until the Present Day,*
**3 vols. Philadelphia: Jewish Publication Society of
America, 1916.**

Volume 3 contains extensive information on Poland, including its various partitions by foreign powers and the
Jewish experience in Poland.

Grossman, Mendel. *With a Camera in the Ghetto.* **New
York: Schocken Books, 1977.**

An extraordinary collection of photographs of the Lodz
Ghetto. An introduction explains Grossman's role in
chronicling the Holocaust and gives important basic statistics about the ghetto and the destruction of the Jews.

Gutman, Yisrael. *The Jews of Warsaw, 1939–1943:
Ghetto, Underground, Revolt.* **Bloomington: Indiana
University Press, 1982.**

Includes notes and bibliography.

Heller, Celia S. *On the Edge of Destruction: Jews of Poland Between the Two World Wars.* **New York: Columbia University Press, 1977.**

Chapters on the country's record of tolerance and hate, the social definition of Jews in Poland, the pattern of oppression, organized terror and abuse, the fate of orthodox Jews, assimilated Jews, those caught between tradition and assimilation, and the Jewish resistance to oppression.

Hilberg, Raul; Staron, Stanislaw; and Kermisz, Josef, eds. *The Warsaw Diary of Adam Czedrniakow: Prelude to Doom.* **New York: Stein and Day, 1979.**

The diary of one of the Warsaw Ghetto leaders. An intimate record of both the German annihilation of the Jews and of the Jewish community's response. Includes a map of the Warsaw Ghetto and a documentary appendix providing some of the primary evidence of the systematic destruction of the Polish Jews.

Huberband, Rabbi Shimon. *Kiddush Hashem: Jewish Religious and Cultural Life in Poland During the Holocaust.* **New York: Yeshiva University Press, 1987.**

Extensive references to Jewish life in Poland, the seizure of Jews in Warsaw in 1942, and life in the ghetto.

Irwin-Zarecka, Iwona. *Neutralizing Memory: The Jew in Contemporary Poland.* **New Brunswick, NJ: Transaction Publishers, 1989.**

Chapters on how the past still informs Poland's present, the way Jews are remembered in Poland, and how those memories are stimulated and dealt with. Includes a note on Polish names and a bibliography.

Katz, Alfred. *Poland's Ghettos at War.* **New York: Twayne, 1970.**

Chapters on Jewish parties and politics in Poland between World Wars I and II, the establishment of Jewish ghettos and their internal organization, the underground resistance to the Nazis, and Polish-Jewish relations during World War II. Includes notes, references, and bibliography.

Korczak, Janusz. *Ghetto Diary*. New York: Holocaust Library, 1978.

A diary kept mainly between May and August 1942.

Kotlar, Helen. *We Lived in a Grave*. New York: Shengold Publishers, 1980.

Details the sudden Nazi attacks, the effort to salvage precious possessions such as religious books, the Jewish Council set up in the ghetto, Nazi exploitation, and the different reactions of Poles to the Jewish plight. Several illustrations.

Krall, Hanna. *Shielding the Flame: An Intimate Conversation with Dr. Marek Edelman, The Last Surviving Leader of the Warsaw Ghetto Uprising*. New York: Henry Holt, 1977.

In an introduction, the distinguished journalist Timothy Garton Ash gives a concise history of Jews and Poles and the impact that Edelman's memoirs have had on a new generation of Poles wanting to know the truth about the Jewish experience in Poland during the war.

Kugelmass, Jack, and Boyarin, Jonathan. *From a Ruined Garden: The Memorial Books of Polish Jewry*. New York: Schocken Books, 1983.

Selections from more than sixty memorial books written by Polish Jews to commemorate their dead. The book has sections on towns, townspeople, lifeways, events, legends, folklore, Holocaust, and the return to Poland. Includes a bibliography, geographical index, and gazetteer.

Lanzmann, Claude. *Shoah: An Oral History of the Holocaust. The Complete Text of the Film*. New York: Pantheon Books, 1985.

Lanzmann's controversial documentary of the concentration camps in Poland. This is one of the major works on the fate of the Jews in Poland and must be read and seen by anyone coming to terms with Polish history.

Lerski, George J., and Lerski, Halina T. *Jewish-Polish Coexistence, 1772–1939: A Topical Bibliography.* **Westport, CT: Greenwood Press, 1986.**

Chapters on selected reference works, general works, periods of Polish partition, Jews in independent Poland, Jews in Polish literature, theater, autobiographies, memoirs, correspondence, biographies, and biographical materials.

Marcus, Joseph. *Social and Political History of the Jews in Poland, 1919–1939.* **Amsterdam: Mouton Publishers, 1983.**

Contains notes, bibliography, and index.

Meed, Vladka. *On Both Sides of the Wall: Memoirs from the Warsaw Ghetto.* **New York: Holocaust Library, 1979.**

A record of ghetto life, the resistance, informers, Polish friends, Jews in hiding, the labor camps, and the author's return to Poland thirty-three years after the war.

Milton, Sybil, ed. *The Stroop Report: The Jewish Quarter of Warsaw Is No More!* **New York: Pantheon Books, 1979.**

The Nazi record of the extermination of the Jews used in evidence at the Nuremberg trials.

Niezabitowska, Malgorzata. *Remnants: The Last Jews of Poland.* **New York: Friendly Press, 1986.**

Only about 5,000 Jews are left in Poland; this is an illustrated chronicle of their lives and history. Includes chronology and glossary.

Schupack, Joseph. *The Dead Years.* **New York: Holocaust Library, 1986.**

Examines Jewish life in Poland before the war, the German invasion, the fate of Schupack's relatives, transports to the concentration camps, and life in the Warsaw Ghetto. Includes a glossary of foreign words.

Singer, Isaac Bashevis. *The Certificate.* **New York: Farrar, Straus & Giroux, 1992.**

Penniless and lonely, eighteen-year-old David Bendiger arrives in Warsaw from his Polish village, searching for love, work, and the meaning of his life.

———. *The Collected Stories.* **New York: Farrar, Straus & Giroux, 1982.**

The life's work of a Nobel Prize-winning Polish Jew, whose writings usually center on his early years in Poland (1908–1918).

———. *A Day of Pleasure: Stories of a Boy Growing Up in Warsaw.* **New York: Farrar, Straus & Giroux, 1969.**

Singer's reminiscences, with poignant photographs by Roman Vishniac.

———. *The Family Moskat.* **New York: Farrar, Straus & Giroux, 1950.**

A wonderful evocation of life in Warsaw just before World War II, showing the enormous variety and vitality of Polish Jews.

———. *In My Father's Court.* **New York: Farrar, Straus & Giroux, 1966.**

Memories of Warsaw, focused on Singer's father, a rabbi in a poor quarter of the city.

———. *The Manor* and *The Estate.* **New York: Avon Books, 1979.**

Singer's great chronicle of a Jewish family struggling to survive in Poland and in New York City.

———. *Satan in Goray*. **New York: Farrar, Straus & Giroux, 1955.**

In seventeenth-century Poland, a little town in Goray awaits the coming of the Jewish messiah.

Smolar, Aleksander. "Jews as a Polish Problem." *Daedalus: A Journal of the American Academy of Arts and Sciences*, **Vol. 116, Spring, 1987, pp. 31–73.**

A discussion of efforts to remove Jews from the study of Polish history. When charged with anti-Semitism, Poles have pointed to their tradition of national and religious tolerance. Yet Jews have often regarded Polish history as a "perpetual process of growing anti-Semitism." Large numbers of Jews emigrated from Poland to escape persecution. Each side, Smolar argues, tends to exaggerate its position.

Strom, Yale. *A Tree Still Stands: Jewish Youth in Eastern Europe Today*. **New York: Putnam, 1990.**

Photo essays of young Jews, all of whom have parents or grandparents who survived the Holocaust.

Uris, Leon. *Mila 18*. **New York: Doubleday, 1961.**

A novel of the Warsaw uprising.

Vinecour, Earl. *Polish Jews: The Final Chapter*. **New York: McGraw-Hill, 1977.**

A brief history of Jews in Poland, as well as a text illustrating historic and contemporary photographs by Chuck Fishman.

Vishniac, Roman. *Polish Jews: A Pictorial History*. **New York: Schocken Books, 1965.**

Photographs of Jewish communities (primarily Polish) that Vishniac took in 1938, on the eve of World War II.

Most of these people were murdered in the Holocaust and their communities destroyed. In an introductory essay, "The Inner World of the Polish Jew," Abraham Heschel explores the world evoked so palpably in the photographs.

CONTEMPORARY POLAND: LECH WALESA, THE SOLIDARITY PERIOD, AND BEYOND (1979–)

Andrews, Nicholas G. *Poland 1980–81: Solidarity versus the Party.* **Washington, DC: National Defense University Press, 1985.**

Chapters on the Polish crises of 1956, 1968, 1970, and 1976; the summer strikes of 1980, the Communist Party's abandonment of Edvard Gierek, the launching of Solidarity, the influence of the Roman Catholic Church, Soviet and American reactions, the imposition of martial law, and an analysis of the crucial years 1980–1981. Includes a glossary of Polish personalities and a chronology of 1980–1981.

Ascherson, Neal. *The Polish August: The Self-Limiting Revolution.* **New York: Viking, 1981.**

Carefully traces the development of the Solidarity movement's goal to change the Communist state without inciting a violent revolution. Contains a bibliography.

———. *The Struggles for Poland.* **New York: Random House, 1987.**

Chapters tracing the rise and fall of independent Poland (966–1900), its period of independence between the two World Wars, its occupation during World War II, the Stalinist period, the Gomulka years (1956–70), the years of Gierek and the period leading to Solidarity (1970–80), and a final chapter on Solidarity, martial law, and the recent past (1980–86). Contains a bibliography.

Ash, Timothy Garton. *The Polish Revolution: Solidarity.* **New York: Charles Scribner's Sons, 1983.**

Explains why Poland erupted in political dissent in 1980. Part 1 gives a vivid, inside look at the developments of August 1980. Part 2 explores the nature of this political revolution and its impact on the West. Includes a chronology, notes, and bibliography.

Blazyca, George, and Rapacki, Ryszard, eds. *Poland into the 1990s*. **New York: St. Martin's Press, 1991.**

Essays on Polish society after communism, its changing political structure, its current reforms and economic policies, the environment, energy and conservation, agriculture, housing, capital investments, the banking system, the private sector, and foreign trade.

The Book of Lech Walesa. **New York: Simon & Schuster, 1982.**

Essays by various contributors on the life and politics of the electrician who became the leader and symbol of the Solidarity movement. Introduction by Neal Ascherson. Includes notes on contributors and a chronology of modern Poland.

Brandys, Kazimierz. *A Warsaw Diary 1978–1981*. **New York: Random House, 1983.**

An important contemporary novelist and former member of the Communist Party. He was blacklisted in the late 1970s for his outspoken work. His diary is an important political and cultural document about Poland in the years leading up to Solidarity.

Brumberg, Abraham, ed. *Poland: Genesis of a Revolution*. **New York: Random House, 1983.**

Includes essays on Polish history, the Communist Party, the relationship between economics and politics, the intelligentsia, the Church, anti-Semitism, Poland, and Eastern Europe.

Cynkin, Thomas M. *Soviet and American Signaling in the Polish Crisis*. **New York: St. Martin's Press, 1988.**

Begins with a chapter on the Czechoslovak crisis of 1968, a case-study prelude to the way the West responded to the advent of Solidarity and tried to manage the crisis and its relationship with the Soviet Union. Includes notes and bibliography.

Dobbs, Michale; Karol, K. S.; and Trevisan, Dessa. *Poland: Solidarity: Walesa.* **New York: McGraw-Hill, 1981.**

A well-illustrated contemporary history of Poland, exploring the country's development since World War II, Solidarity as a peaceful revolution, and the prominence of Lech Walesa as a symbol of the Polish August.

Gildner, Gary. *The Warsaw Sparks.* **Iowa City: University of Iowa Press, 1990.**

A poet and short-story writer, Gildner spent a year in Poland as a Fulbright Lecturer. He organized a baseball team of twenty-six Poles. This is his memoir of what he learned about Polish culture.

Karpinski, Jakub. *Count-Down: The Polish Upheavals of 1956, 1968, 1970, 1976, 1980...* **New York: Karz-Cohl Publishers, 1982.**

A comprehensive study of how Polish protests against the Communist government and Soviet dominance affected various institutions such as the press, the Church, Catholic and youth associations, and the Party itself and how events elsewhere (such as the 1968 upheaval in Czechoslovakia) were related to evolving resistance to the Communist state.

Kemp-Welch, A. *The Birth of Solidarity: The Gdansk Negotiations, 1980.* **New York: St. Martin's Press, 1983.**

Detailed account of the historic negotiations between the workers and the Communist government, the first time workers had ever been treated as equals by a Communist state. Includes a copy of the agreement, extensive notes, and profiles of the participants.

Kurski, Jaroslaw. *Lech Walesa: Democrat or Dictator?* San Francisco: Westview Press, 1993.

Kurski was press spokesman for Walesa from October 1989 to July 1990. He praises Walesa's many accomplishments but decries the manipulative and authoritarian tendencies that may have put him out of touch with the working people who brought him to power. Includes chronology, suggested readings, and glossary of names.

Laba, Roman. *The Roots of Solidarity: A Political Sociology of Poland's Working-Class Democratization.* Princeton: Princeton University Press, 1991.

Traces the "demystification of the party-state," beginning with the violence in the Polish port city of Gdynia in 1970 and a general strike in another port city, Szczecion, which the author sees as planting the ideological roots of Solidarity as a grass-roots movement. Extensive notes and bibliography.

Lepak, John Keith. *Prelude to Solidarity: Poland and the Politics of the Gierek Regime.* New York: Columbia University Press, 1988.

Explores all aspects of the regime: politics, economics (industrial and agricultural policy), and foreign policy. Includes notes and bibliography.

MacShane, Denis. *Solidarity: Poland's Independent Trade Union.* Nottingham, U.K.: Spokesman, 1981.

Concentrates on the events immediately leading up to the formation of Solidarity in 1980, and then on its political and economic program, as well as the significance of the Gdansk agreement. An appendix includes a detailed explanation of the Nomenklatura, the system by which the Communist Party kept all aspects of power in its grip.

Potel, Jean-Yves. *The Promise of Solidarity: Inside the Polish Workers' Struggle, 1980–82.* **New York: Praeger, 1982.**

Chapters on the workers, the strike, the calls for democracy, the difficulties of negotiating with the Communist government, the impact of Solidarity on the countryside, and its promise for the future. Includes a list of the twenty-one demands issued by Solidarity, notes on notable people and organizations, and a chronology of events.

Rachwald, Arthur R. *In Search of Poland: The Superpowers' Response to Solidarity, 1980–1989.* **Stanford, CA: Hoover Institution Press, 1990.**

Part 1 concentrates on Solidarity and its attempts to fend off the intrusion of the Soviet Union; Part 2 explores Solidarity's relationship with the United States; Part 3 covers the government's banning of Solidarity and its aftermath. Includes notes and bibliography.

Rollyson, Carl. "Freeze-Frame Poland 1979: Polish Cowboys and Marlboro Men." *Icarus,* **Vol. 12, Fall, 1993, pp. 1–11.**

A memoir of Poland in the days just before the first Solidarity strike, and a meditation on the impact of American popular culture on Polish culture.

———. "In Poland." *The Detroit Free Press, Detroit Magazine,* **November 16, 1980, pp. 10–11, 18, 20, 28, 30, 32.**

A firsthand report on everyday life, emphasizing the author's friendships with Poles and their vision of the United States.

Stoppard, Tom. *Squaring the Circle.* **Boston: Faber & Faber, 1984.**

A provocative portrayal of the rise and fall of Solidarity by a renowned playwright.

Touraine, Alain; Dubet, Francois; Wieviorka, Michel; and Strzelecki, Jan. *Solidarity: The Analysis of a Social Movement: Poland 1980–1981.* **Cambridge: Cambridge University Press, 1983.**

> Part 1 details resistance movements in Poland that presaged the 1980 Solidarity strike. Part 2 details the growth of Solidarity and the thrust to end the Communist government. Includes a chronology and bibliography.

Weschler, Lawrence. *Solidarity: Poland in the Season of Its Passion.* **New York: Simon & Schuster, 1982.**

> One of the most vivid firsthand accounts of the birth of Solidarity, filled with revealing anecdotes and explanations of Polish history, including the treatment of the Jews. Includes over fifty photographs of the events, personalities, and documents of the Solidarity period.

Woodal, Jean, ed. *Policy and Politics in Contemporary Poland: Reform, Failure, Crisis.* **New York: St. Martin's Press, 1982.**

> Essays on Socialist society, Poland and Eastern Europe, the role of the Communist leadership, party-state structures, the degeneration of central planning, the development of self-management and new trade unions, and educational and health policy.

Zagajewski, Adam. *Solidarity, Solitude.* **New York: Ecco Press, 1990.**

> A Polish poet writes about his conflicting loyalties: to his work, to the Solidarity movement, a balancing of the "civic" and the "poetic."

AUTOBIOGRAPHY

Fluek, Toby. *My Life in a Polish Village, 1930–1949.* **New York: Knopf, 1990.**

> Using her own paintings and drawings, Fluek evokes her life as a Jew before the war, the Nazi occupation, and her emigration from Poland.

Hautzig, Esther. *The Endless Steppe: Growing Up in Siberia.* **New York: HarperCollins, 1968.**

From the ages of ten to fourteen the author was a Polish deportee living with her mother and grandmother in a remote, impoverished Siberian village during World War II.

Milosz, Czeslaw. *Beginning with My Streets: Essays and Recollections.* **New York: Farrar, Straus & Giroux, 1991.**

Covers his childhood in Lithuania, his career as a poet in the East and the West, and essays on both Polish and American writers.

———. *The Captive Mind.* **New York: Knopf, 1951.**

Reprinted in several paperback editions. One of the classic texts of the early Cold War, explaining conditions in postwar Poland, the grip communism came to have on Eastern European intellectuals, and why Milosz had to leave his country.

Pilsudski, Jozef. *The Memories of a Polish Revolutionary and Soldier.* **London: Faber & Faber, 1931.**

Covers Pilsudski's experiences up to the year 1923—just after his stirring 1920 victory over the Russians that kept Poland an independent state. He is one of the towering figures of Polish history, lionized for his military prowess, often criticized for turning Poland away from its democratic traditions in the 1930s. Includes important illustrations and maps.

———. *Year 1920 and Its Climax: Battle of Warsaw During the Polish-Soviet War 1919–1920.* **New York: Pilsudski Institute of America, 1972.**

The general's account of his victory over the Red Army, a battle that ensured Poland's independence.

Rose, William John, tr. and ed. *From Serfdom to Self-Government: Memoirs of a Polish Village Mayor 1842–1927*. London: Minerva Publishing Co., 1941.

Wonderful insight into Polish life, a firsthand view of life on the land, peasant communities, and public life.

Wat, Aleksander. *My Century: The Odyssey of a Polish Intellectual*. Berkeley: University of California Press, 1988.

The autobiography of one of the great figures of Polish literary history. This is an excellent guide to twentieth-century art and politics in Poland. Contains a useful overview of Wat by Czeslaw Milosz and an introduction by Wat's translator, Richard Lourie.

BIOGRAPHIES OF POLES

Madison, Arnold. *Polish Greats*. New York: David McKay Co., 1980.

Chapters on Copernicus, Kosciuszko, Pulaski, Mickiewicz, Chopin, Conrad, Paderewski, Curie, Rubinstein, and Pope John Paul II.

Thompson, Ewa M. *Witold Gombrowicz*. Boston: Twayne, 1979.

An introduction to a major twentieth-century writer, with chapters on his life, short stories, plays, novels, and memoirs, as well as on his use of language, treatment of women, and relationships with other writers. Includes notes, bibliography, and index.

Yurieff, Zoya. *Joseph Wittlin*. Boston: Twayne, 1973.

An introduction to an important novelist, poet, essayist, and translator, best known for his World War I novel *The Salt of the Earth*. He is the first Polish writer to receive the award of the American Academy of Arts and Letters. "Anyone who does not know Wittlin does not know Polish literature," says Yurieff, quoting a German critic.

Joseph Conrad (Jozef Konrad Korzeniowski)

Morf, Gustav. *The Polish Shades of Joseph Conrad*. New York: Astra Books, 1976.

A study of Conrad's Polish background and what it contributed to his English novels.

Najder, Zdzislaw. *Joseph Conrad: A Chronicle*. New Brunswick, NJ: Rutgers University Press, 1984.

Chapter 1 details Conrad's Polish upbringing and background, and Chapter 13 tells of his last trip to Poland on the eve of World War I.

Frederic Chopin

Liszt, Franz. *Frederic Chopin*. New York: Vienna House, 1963.

Chapters on the social background of Chopin's famous compositions and on his youth in Poland. Edward N. Waters provides an introduction explaining the friendship between the two famous composers and performers.

Marek, George R., and Gordon-Smith, Maria. *Chopin*. New York: Harper & Row, 1978.

A recent, crisply written biography that attempts to correct the chauvinism of Polish authors as well as the lack of familiarity with Polish history shown by Chopin's non-Polish biographers. Marek's coauthor was born Maria Krystyna Broniewska in Warsaw and was educated there. Includes a Chopin Calendar (his life and works, political, social, and artistic events of his time), and a bibliography.

Mizwa, Stephen P., ed. *Frederic Chopin*. Westport, CT: Greenwood Press, 1983. [First published in 1949.]

A collection of essays, including "Chopin's Indebtedness to the Artistic Tradition of Music in Poland" and "The Most Polish of Polish Composers."

Wierzynski, Casimir. *The Life and Death of Chopin.* **New York: Simon & Schuster, 1949.**

A lively, well-paced narrative written by a Pole.

Marie Curie

Brandt, Keith. *Marie Curie, Brave Scientist.* **Mahwah, NJ: Troll Associates, 1983.**

A brief illustrated biography focusing on the youth of the scientist who twice received the Nobel Prize for her work with radium.

Curie, Eve. *Madame Curie: A Biography.* **New York: Doubleday, 1937.**

A well-illustrated biography of the famous Polish scientist by her daughter. Her prizes, medals, decorations, and honorary titles are listed in an appendix.

Parker, Steve. *Marie Curie and Radium.* **New York: HarperCollins, 1992.**

The life and work of Marie Curie from childhood to the discovery of radium and her two Nobel prizes.

Quinn, Susan. *Marie Curie: A Life.* **New York: Simon & Schuster, 1995.**

A comprehensive biography based on available documents translated from the Polish for the first time. Quinn manages to capture both the warmth and genius of her remarkable subject and to explore her extraordinary scientific achievements.

Pope John Paul II (Karol Wojtyla)

Craig, Mary. *Man from a Far Country: An Informal Portrait of Pope John Paul II.* **New York: Morrow, 1979.**

A brief biography based on firsthand research in Poland. Includes bibliography.

His Holiness John Paul II. *Crossing the Threshold of Hope.* **New York: Knopf, 1994.**

Pope John Paul II discusses the existence of God, the dignity of man, pain, suffering, hope, and other questions of faith.

Johnson, Paul. *Pope John Paul II and the Catholic Restoration.* **New York: St. Martin's Press, 1981.**

A look at how the Polish background of the pope shaped his route to the papacy.

Malinski, Mieczyslaw. *Pope John Paul II: The Life of Karol Wojtyla.* **New York: Seabury Press, 1980.**

Organized around the event of his becoming Pope, with flashbacks to his experiences in Nazi-occupied Poland, his life in the postwar Communist period, his career in Rome, his term as Bishop Wojtyla, and his work as pope.

Szulc, Tad. *Pope John Paul II: The Biography.* **New York: Scribner, 1995.**

An unauthorized biography based on interviews with the pope. Szulc provides a sympathetic and probing biography, examining the pope's conservatism and his role as a critic of capitalist society and champion of religious freedom. The biographer also provides fascinating material on Wojtyla's early years in Poland, his role in the Polish underground, and his rise in the Polish church.

Tadeusz Kosciuszko

Haiman, Miecislaus. *Kosciuszko in the American Revolution.* **New York: Polish Institute of Arts and Sciences in America, 1943.**

Covers the two major periods of Kosciuszko's involvement with the United States—during the Revolutionary War (1776–1784) and a later visit (1797–1798). Includes illustrations, maps, and bibliography.

Wieczerzak, Joseph. "Pre- and Proto-Ethnics: Poles in the United States before the Immigration 'After Bread'." *Polish Review,* **Vol. 21, 1976, p. 12.**

Wieczerzak examines the impact of Polish American patriots such as Kosciuszko and Pulaski on later Polish immigrants. He speculates that Kosciuszko and Pulaski heightened American sympathies toward Polish immigrants and provided these same immigrants with the feeling that they had roots in the United States, thereby easing the process of assimilation.

Ignacy Jan Paderewski

Hoskins, Janina W. *Ignacy Jan Paderewski 1860–1941: A Biographical Sketch and a Selective List of Reading Materials*. Washington, DC: Library of Congress, 1984.

As Hoskins notes, Paderewski is a "unique figure in modern Polish history." A brilliant concert pianist and composer, he became a prominent statesman and spokesman for the cause of an independent Poland.

Joseph Pilsudski

Dziewanowski, M. K. *Joseph Pilsudski: A European Federalist, 1918–1922*. Stanford: Hoover Institution Press, 1969.

The author considers 1918–1922 to be the peak of Pilsudski's career, when he won independence for Poland and worked to establish a federal system in Europe. He notes that this period has been overshadowed by the last years of Pilsudski's rule in Poland, when he became a virtual dictator.

Jedrzejewicz, Waclaw. *Pilsudski: A Life for Poland*. New York: Hippocrene Books, 1982.

Contains an introduction by Zbigniew Brzezinski, who notes that this is the first biography in English of Pilsudski in forty-three years. Yet an understanding of his life is essential to an understanding of modern Poland. Indeed there was a cult of support for Pilsudski among some of the Solidarity activists, for he preserved Poland during the

Soviet invasion. Yet, he failed to create a multinational commonwealth "based on principles of social justice and ethnic tolerance, to which he aspired in his youth." Jedrzejewicz joined Pilsudski's legion as a young man and served in top-level diplomatic positions.

Casimir Pulaski

Manning, Clarence A. *Soldier of Liberty: Casimir Pulaski.* **New York: Philosophical Library, 1945.**

A lively biography of the Polish hero who died at the age of thirty-two, mortally wounded at the battle of Savannah in the American Revolutionary War.

Mocha, Frank, ed. *Poles in America: Bicentennial Essays.* **Stevens Point, WI: Worzalla Publishing Co., 1978.**

Essays on the history of the first Poles in America, including Pulaski.

POLISH LITERATURE AND ART

Baranczak, Stanislaw. *Breathing Under Water and Other East European Essays.* **Cambridge: Harvard University Press, 1990.**

An impressive collection of essays on East European literature and politics.

Borski, Lucia Merecka. *The Jolly Tailor and Other Fairy Tales from the Polish.* **New York: Longmans, 1928.**

The stories are representative of Polish folklore. Includes illustrations and glossary.

Coleman, Marion Moor. *Our Other World: A Polish Scrapbook.* **Cheshire, CT: Cherry Hill Books, n.d.**

Chapters on early Polish history, on literary figures such as Mickiewicz, Reymont, and Sienkiewicz, on Poles abroad, on musical figures, and on aspects of the Polish experience in the United States.

Lednicki, Waclaw. *Life and Culture of Poland as Reflected in Polish Literature.* **New York: Roy, 1944.**

Chapters on interpretations of Polish history, political ideals, religion and national life, squires and peasants, the national poet (Adam Mickiewicz), Poland under the partitions, and Polish traits. Contains a bibliography.

Mayewski, Pawel, ed. *The Broken Mirror: A Collection of Writings from Contemporary Poland.* **New York: Random House, 1958.**

Important work by Tadeusz Rozewicz, Zbigniew Herbert, Leszek Kolakowski, and others, with an introduction by the distinguished American critic Lionel Trilling. Includes biographical notes.

Milosz, Czeslaw. *The History of Polish Literature*, **2d ed. Berkeley and Los Angeles: University of California Press, 1983.**

A comprehensive narrative history by Poland's Nobel Prize-winning poet. Milosz, who emigrated to the United States after World War II, covers every period from the Middle Ages to the twentieth century. He also provides in-depth biographies of major writers and literary movements. Includes an essay on Polish versification and a bibliography.

Minczeski, John, ed. *Concert at Chopin's House: A Collection of Polish-American Writing.* **St. Paul, MN: New Rivers Press, 1987.**

Collection of poetry with an introduction on Polish American writers and photographs.

Stankiewicz, W. J., ed. *The Tradition of Polish Ideals: Essays in History and Literature.* **London: Orbis Books, 1981.**

Chapters on Polish identity, tolerance in Poland, the Polish nobility, Copernicus, Chopin, Sienkewicz, the Warsaw uprising, the Polish playwright Slawomir Mrozek, and postwar Polish poets.

Fiction

Borowski, Tadeusz. *This Way for the Gas, Ladies and Gentlemen.* **New York: Penguin Books, 1976.**

> A paperback reprint of the author's concentration camp stories. First published in Poland after World War II, the volume is one of the key works about the Holocaust. This edition includes an introduction by the distinguished Polish critic Jan Kott.

Konwicki, Tadeusz. *The Polish Complex.* **New York: Farrar, Straus & Giroux, 1982.**

> A novel published in Poland in 1977, just a few years before the first Solidarity strikes. It provides revealing portraits of everyday life in a society on the eve of momentous changes.

Lem, Stanislaw. *Solaris.* **New York: Berkeley Medallion Books, 1971.**

> Perhaps the most famous novel by Poland's premier science fiction novelist. Several of his science fiction novels have been published in English and hailed by critics as classics of the genre.

Michener, James A. *Poland.* **New York: Random House, 1983.**

> A novel that deals with the whole of Polish history, the book is framed by contemporary events in 1981, then delves into the Polish experience of World Wars I and II, before exploring the country's rich medieval heritage.

Morska, Irena, ed. *Polish Authors of Today and Yesterday.* **New York: S. F. Vanni, 1947.**

> A selection of nineteenth- and twentieth-century short stories. The preface and introduction give a capsule history of Polish literary history, with notes on individual authors such as Boleslaw Prus, Wladyslaw Reymont, Henryk Sienkiewicz, and Stefan Zeromski.

Schultz, Bruno. *The Street of Crocodiles*. New York: Penguin Books, 1977.

First published in Poland in 1934, this is a memorable record of Jewish life in Poland. Schultz was killed by the Nazis in 1942.

Styron, William. *Sophie's Choice*. New York: Random House, 1979.

The novel is narrated by a callow Southern youth, Stingo, who becomes involved in the lives of Sophie, a Polish immigrant, and her erratic lover, Nathan, a Jewish American. Through Stingo's obsession with Sophie, he learns much about the Holocaust and the terrible choice Sophie had to make in a concentration camp. Styron joins major aspects of both the American and Polish/European experiences. The novel was made into a major motion picture with a stunning performance by Meryl Streep as Sophie.

Poetry

Baranczak, Stanislaw. *A Fugitive from Utopia*. Cambridge: Harvard University Press, 1987.

A sensitive study of Zbigniew Herbert, whom Baranczak calls the "most admired and respected poet now living in Poland."

Baranczak, Stanislaw, and Cavanagh, Clare. *Polish Poetry of the Last Two Decades of Communist Rule*. Evanston, IL: Northwestern University Press, 1991.

Contains work of the major poets of this period, with notes on the poems and biographies of the poets.

Carpenter, Bogdana, ed. *Monumenta Polonica: The First Four Centuries of Polish Poetry: A Bilingual Anthology*. Ann Arbor: Michigan Slavic Publications, 1989.

In addition to comprehensive selections of poets from the Middle Ages to the Enlightenment, the volume contains introductions, notes, bibliography, and many illustrations.

Dusza, Edward L. *Poets of Warsaw Aflame.* **Stevens Point: University of Wisconsin–Stevens Point Foundation, 1977.**

A study of the wartime poetry of Poland's underground writers. Includes notes and bibliography.

Gillon, Adam, ed. *Poems of the Ghetto: A Testament of Lost Men.* **New York: Twayne, 1969.**

Parts 1 and 2 present poems written in the Warsaw Ghetto, with brief notes on each poet. Part 3 contains poems by those spared the horrors of the ghetto and the concentration camps. Several poems are illustrated.

Gomori, George. *Polish and Hungarian Poetry 1945 to 1956.* **Oxford: Oxford University Press, 1966.**

Discusses the historical and social role of the poet in Poland and Hungary. Explores Polish poetic models, Polish poetry just before, during, and after World War II and the younger generation (represented by Rozewicz), the influence of communism on poets, and the relaxation of political controls on poets in the mid-1950s.

Herbert, Zbigniew. *Selected Poems.* **New York: Ecco Press, 1986.**

Considered one of Poland's greatest contemporary poets. Contains an excellent introduction by the distinguished critic A. Alvarez.

Levine, Madeline. *Contemporary Polish Poetry 1925–1975.* **Boston: Twayne, 1981.**

Contains a chronology, chapters on individual poets such as Milosz, Rozewicz, and Herbert, notes, and selected bibliography.

Adam Mickiewicz

Gardner, Monica M. *Adam Mickiewicz: The National*

Poet of Poland. **New York: Arno Press, 1971. [First published in 1911.]**

Not a full biography but a sketch of his life and career in nineteenth-century Europe. Includes chapters on his major works and a bibliography.

Mills, Clark, ed. *Adam Mickiewicz. Selected Poems 1798–1855.* **New York: Noonday Press, 1956.**

Includes introductory notes, critical appreciation, and selected bibliography.

Simmons, Ernest J., ed. *Adam Mickiewicz: Poet of Poland.* **New York: Columbia University Press, 1951.**

A symposium on the poet and his work. Articles on historical and biographical data, his poetic masterpiece *Pan Tadeusz,* his reception in the United States and friendships with American writers such as James Fenimore Cooper, Margaret Fuller, and Ralph Waldo Emerson.

Czeslaw Milosz

Czarnecka, Ewa, and Fiut, Aleksander. *Conversations with Czeslaw Milosz.* **New York: Harcourt Brace Jovanovich, 1987.**

Covers much of the poet's life and writings, with chapters on his individual works and topics that span many pieces. Includes a detailed chronology.

Milosz, Czeslaw. *The Collected Poems 1931–1987.* **New York: Ecco Press, 1988.**

Contains a brief preface and notes commenting on individual poems.

————. *Postwar Polish Poetry: An Anthology,* **3d ed. Los Angeles: University of California Press, 1983.**

Presents 125 poems by twenty-five poets, including those now living outside Poland but still in active contact with their Polish contemporaries.

Nathan, Leonard, and Quinn, Arthur. *The Poet's Work: An Introduction to Czeslaw Milosz*. Cambridge: Harvard University Press, 1991.

> A solid study by two of Milosz's colleagues at the University of California. Includes notes and bibliography.

Drama

Czerwinski, E. J. *Pieces of Poland: Four Polish Dramatists*. Long Island, NY: Slavic and Eastern European Arts, 1983.

> Gabriela Zapolska, Stanislaw Grochowiak, Eugeniusz Priwieziencew, and Tadeusz Rozewicz are the four playwrights represented. Includes notes on the production history and style of each writer's plays.

Mrozek, Slawomir. *Six Plays by Slawomir Mrozek*. New York: Grove Press, 1967.

> An excellent anthology of work by Poland's premier playwright. His plays are masterful parodies of politics.

Rozewicz, Tadeusz. *The Card Index and Other Plays*. New York: Grove Press, 1969.

> Three plays with a brief author's introduction. In subtle ways, each drama is about the restriction of liberty in Poland under the Communist regime—although politics is not the explicit subject.

Segel, Harold B., ed. *Polish Romantic Drama: Three Plays in English Translation*. Ithaca: Cornell University Press, 1977.

> An introduction and selections from plays by Adam Mickiewicz, Zygmunt Krasinski, and Juliusz Slowacki. Contains a bibliography.

Witkiewicz, Stanislaw Ignacy. *The Madman and the Nun and Other Plays*. Seattle: University of Washington Press, 1968.

A world-class playwright, his work has been compared to the Theater of the Absurd tradition of Beckett, Ionesco, and Genet.

————. *Tropical Madness*. **New York: Winter House, 1972.**

Four plays by one of Poland's greatest avant-garde playwrights. Includes an introductory essay, "The Search for a Metaphysical Dimension in Drama," by Martin Esslin, one of the foremost critics of modern drama.

Film

Cameron, Ian. *Second Wave*. **New York: Praeger, 1970.**

Interviews with contemporary directors, with a chapter on Jerzy Skolimowski.

Goulding, Daniel J., ed. *Five Filmmakers: Tarkovsky, Forman, Polanski, Szabo, Makavejev*. **Bloomington: Indiana University Press, 1994.**

Contains a chapter on Roman Polanski. Contains a bibliography.

Leaming, Barbara. *Polanski: A Biography*. **New York: Simon & Schuster, 1981.**

An unauthorized biography of an important film director, tracing his sufferings in Poland during World War II and his subsequent success as a precocious filmmaker who eventually achieved renown as one of the finest contemporary filmmakers. Includes illustrations and filmography.

Roud, Richard. *Cinema: A Critical Dictionary*. **London: Secker and Warburg, 1980.**

Contains essays on major Polish filmmakers: "Roman Polanski, Jerzy Skolimowski, and the Polish Émigrés," "Polish Cinema Since the War," "Walerian Borowczyk," and "Krzysztof Zanussi."

Thomson, David. *A Biographical Dictionary of Film*, **3d ed. New York: Knopf, 1994.**

Entries on Walerian Borowczyk, Krzysztof Kieslowski, Jerzy Skolimowski, Roman Polanski, and Andrzej Wajda.

Tuska, Jon. *Encounters with Filmmakers: Eight Career Studies.* **Westport, CT: Greenwood Press, 1991.**

Interview with Roman Polanski.

Wajda, Andrzej. *Double Vision: My Life in Film.* **New York: Henry Holt, 1989.**

The noted Polish director's account of his career in film. Filmography and author's biographical notes on select important figures in his text.

NOTABLE POLISH AMERICANS AND BOOKS BY AND ABOUT POLISH AMERICANS

Abramson, Harold J. *Ethnic Diversity in Catholic America.* **New York: John Wiley Sons, 1973.**

Extensive references to Poland and Polish Americans.

Budrewicz, Olgierd. *The Melting-Pot Revisited.* **Warsaw: Interpress, 1977.**

Chapters on mathematicians (Stanislaw Ulam), a mayor of Detroit (Roman Gribbs), a Watergate prosecutor (Leon Jaworski), a baseball player (Stan Musial), and several others. Illustrated.

Nelson Algren

Although not a Polish American, and not usually considered an ethnic writer, Algren's novels are filled with portraits of Polish Americans.

The Man with The Golden Arm. **Garden City, NY: Doubleday, 1949.**

The Neon Wilderness. **Gloucester, MA: Peter Smith, 1968.**

Never Come Morning. **New York: Harper, 1942. (Reprinted 1969.)**

Richard Bankowski

His novels follow the fortunes of a Polish American family, the Macheks, immigrants from a village near Lublin. Set in New Jersey, Pennsylvania, New York City, and the Southwest.

After Pentecost. New York: Random House, 1961.

A Glass Rose. New York: Random House, 1958.

On a Dark Night. New York: Random House, 1964.

The Pale Criminals. New York: Random House, 1967.

Saul Bellow

The Adventures of Augie March. New York: Viking, 1953.

> Set in 1930s Chicago, this novel portrays its Jewish protagonist's interactions with neighborhood Poles.

Zbigniew Brzezinski

President Carter's national security adviser and a distinguished historian and analyst of global politics, Brzezinski was born in Warsaw in 1928.

The Grand Failure: The Birth and Death of Communism in the Twentieth Century. New York: Scribner, 1989.

> See Chapter 9, "Polish Society's Self-Emancipation."

Out of Control: Global Turmoil on the Eve of the Twenty-First Century. New York: Charles Scribner's Sons, 1993.

> An ambitious account of twentieth-century history, what the author calls a century of megadeath, coercive utopias, and geopolitical vacuums. Brzezinski calls for a comprehensive examination of global change leading to the

twenty-first century and of the United States's role in it. He calls this the "postutopian age," a time when the seductions of ideologies such as communism have been vanquished but have not been replaced by any over-arching system of beliefs. Numerous references to Poles and post-Communist Poland.

Power and Principle: Memoirs of the National Security Adviser 1977–1981. New York: Farrar, Straus & Giroux, 1983.

Specific references to Poland.

The Soviet Bloc: Unity and Conflict. Cambridge: Harvard University Press, 1960.

See Chapter 11, "The Polish October: The Challenge of Domesticism." Includes bibliography.

Stuart Dybek

Like Algren in subject matter, Dybek writes about Chicago's Polish Americans, but with more concern for their ethnic consciousness and sense of place.

"Autobiography." Poetry, December, 1968, pp. 161–164.

"Blight." Chicago, October, 1985, pp. 193–249.

Childhood and Other Neighborhoods. New York: Viking, 1986.

"Chopin in Winter." Chicago, March, 1984, pp. 154–166.

"Hot Ice" in The Coast of Chicago. New York: Knopf, 1990.

"The Immigrant." Porch, Vol. 2, Summer/Fall, 1979, p. 18.

"The Writer in Chicago." Tri-Quarterly, Vol. 60, 1984, pp. 325–347.

Otto Feinstein
Ethnic Groups in the City: Culture, Institutions, and Power. **Lexington, MA: Heath Lexington Books, 1971.**

> Chapter 12, "The Changing Role of the Polish American," and Chapter 31, "New Experiment in the Schools," discuss the way the Polish American experience has been taught in the curriculum of Orchard Lake, Michigan, schools. Several other chapters deal with the Polish American contribution to the city of Detroit.

Gary Gildner
Draws on his family's Polish past in both his poetry and fiction. His later work reflects the impact of his experience as a Fulbright Lecturer at the University of Warsaw. Ethnicity itself becomes the subject of his work.

Blue Like the Heavens. **Pittsburgh: University of Pittsburgh Press, 1984.**

First Practice. **Pittsburgh: University of Pittsburgh Press, 1969.**

"In a Warsaw Classroom Containing Chairs." *Grand Street,* **Vol. 8, Winter, 1989, pp. 157–159.**

Nails. **Pittsburgh: University of Pittsburgh Press, 1975.**

"Primarily We Miss Ourselves as Children." *River Styx,* **Vol. 29, Winter, 1989, p. 66.**

The Second Bridge. **Chapel Hill: Algonquin, 1987.**

"String." *Poetry,* **December, 1988, p. 127.**

"To Live in Warsaw." *Georgia Review,* **Vol. 42, Fall, 1988, pp. 605–606.**

The Warsaw Sparks. **Iowa City: University of Iowa Press, 1990.**

Thomas S. Gladsky
Princes, Peasants, and Other Polish Selves: Ethnicity in American Literature. Amherst: University of Massachusetts Press, 1992.

Part 1, "Polish Selves—American Perspectives," explores how Polish writers invented the "beau ideal" of the Polish patriot and hero, the creations of a Polish literary self from 1880 to 1930, the saga of the immigrants, Polish involvement in proletarian movements and literature, the World War II period, and attitudes of Jewish American writers toward Poland. Part 2, "American Selves—Ethnic Perspective," discusses the reconstruction of ethnicity by Polish American writers and what it means to be Polish American today. Includes bibliography.

Antoni Gronowicz
An immigrant writer, he celebrates the Polish tie to the United States, but he also criticizes American industry for exploiting workers.

Bolek. New York: Thomas Nelson and Sons, 1942.

A comprehensive portrayal of Polish and American kinship. Explores the experiences of Poles in Chicago and Pittsburgh and evokes the Poles' sense of the United States as the promised land.

Four from the Old Town. New York: Scribner, 1994.

Set in the Polish city of Lwow, the novel covers the years 1939–1944. The author also explores the tensions between Christian, Jewish, and Ukrainian Poles in the prewar period.

Jerzy Kosinski
Although born in Poland, the Jewish Kosinski has not been considered a Polish writer. He resisted identification as a Pole, a Jew, or an ethnic writer. Yet as critic Thomas

Gladsky observes, Kosinski's novels are "unmistakably ethnic. They deal invariably with the Cold War immigrant self, adjusting . . . to a new American culture and to an old Polish one." Many of his protagonists have Eastern European backgrounds and are political refugees. Kosinski often presents Poland in a harsh light, but his later work reveals his groping for a reconciliation with his native land.

Blind Date. **Boston: Houghton Mifflin, 1977.**

> Like Tarden in *Cockpit,* Levanter is a transplanted Slav, using his position in an intelligence agency to wreak vengeance on Eastern Europe's totalitarian regimes.

Cockpit. **New York: Houghton Mifflin, 1975.**

> The main character, Tarden, grapples with his roots in Poland, trying to align his understanding of past and present.

The Hermit of 69th Street. **New York: Henry Holt, 1988.**

> Kosinski's hero, Norbert Kosky, seems modeled after himself—an exiled Polish writer living in the United States and wrestling with his rootlessness and alienation. Poland and Polish culture receive much greater play—indeed Kosinski appears positively patriotic, contradicting the bitter attacks he lodged against his native land in his other novels.

The Painted Bird. **Boston: Houghton Mifflin, 1965.**

> Set in Poland during World War II and based, in part, on the author's own experience among sadistic Polish peasants, this novel brought Kosinski an international reputation.

Passion Play. **New York: St. Martin's Press, 1979.**

> Fabian is another Slavic protagonist who resents his past in Eastern Europe, where his playmates often "turned on him in the bond and unity of their family kinship." Like

many Kosinski characters, he is an outsider and an immigrant.

Pinball. New York: Bantam, 1982.

The clearest example of Kosinski's effort to reconcile with his Eastern European heritage. His criticism seems benign, sometimes comical, and his hero, Patrick Domostroy, lacks the avenging fury of Kosinski's previous protagonists.

Steps. New York: Random House, 1968.

Continues Kosinski's excoriating look at Poland, especially its postwar Socialist culture.

Books about Jerzy Kosinski

Cronin, Gloria L. *Jerzy Kosinski: An Annotated Bibliography*. Westport, CT: Greenwood Press, 1991.

Lavers, Norman. *Jerzy Kosinski*. Boston: Twayne, 1982.

Critical study of an important contemporary writer, detailing his life in Poland during World War II, his early sociological works, and his success as a novelist writing in English. Includes chronology, notes, and bibliography.

Lupack, Barbara Tepa. *Plays of Passion, Games of Chance: Jerzy Kosinski and His Fiction*. Bristol, IN: Wyndham Hall Press, 1988.

Contains notes and a bibliography.

Teicholz, Tom, ed. *Conversations with Jerzy Kosinski*. Jackson: University Press of Mississippi, 1993.

Published interviews collected from magazines.

Walsh, Thomas. *John Barth, Jerzy Kosinski, and Thomas Pynchon: A Reference Guide*. Boston: G. K. Hall, 1977.

Bibliography of books and articles by Kosinski and writings about Kosinski, 1960–1973.

Anne Pellowski

Author of a tetralogy of novels for younger readers about Polish American life on a Wisconsin farm. The Pellowski family adapts its Polish background to the United States, and the United States profits from their industry. Polish customs and wistful memories of Poland pervade the stories.

***First Farm in the Valley.* New York: Philomel, 1982.**

Includes a pronunciation guide and family tree.

***Stair Step Farm.* New York: Philomel, 1981.**

***Willow Wind Farm.* New York: Philomel, 1981.**

***Winding Valley Farm.* New York: Philomel, 1982.**

Darryl Ponicsan

Several of his novels follow the fortunes of the Budduskys, social rebels whose behavior reflects Ponicsan's satire of American society.

***The Accomplice.* New York: Harper & Row, 1975.**

Beef Buddusky, a misfit, goes from prison to odd jobs and from one failed relationship to another.

***Andoshen, Pa.* New York: Dial Press, 1973.**

A Polish mining town in northeastern Pennsylvania buffeted by the rapid changes taking place in the 1960s and 1970s.

***Goldengrove.* New York: Dial Press, 1971.**

Ernie Buddusky struggles to maintain his middle-class status.

***The Last Detail.* New York: Dial Press, 1970.**

Emphasizes the Buddusky rebelliousness and refusal to kowtow to the system—in this case the military.

General John Shalikashvili

General Shalikashvili is the subject of innumerable articles, among which are the following:

Fisher, David. "A Diplomat's Soldier." *San Francisco Chronicle,* August 13, 1993, Section A, p. 23.

Kranish, Michael. "General Picked to Be Chairman of Joint Chiefs." *Boston Globe,* August 12, 1993, Section 1, p. 1.

Luttwak, Edward N. "Shalikashvili Brings Back Balance." *Los Angeles Times,* August 16, 1993, Section B, p. 7.

Leon Uris

Mila 18. New York: Doubleday, 1961.

> A novel of the Warsaw uprising.

OBVII. Garden City, NY: Doubleday, 1970.

> Set in the concentration camps of Poland.

POLISH AMERICANS IN THEATER

Williams, Tennessee. *A Streetcar Named Desire.* New York: New Directions, 1947.

> Features one of the most famous Polish Americans in American literature, Stanley Kowalski.

POLISH AMERICANS IN FILM

Miller, Randall M., ed. *The Kaleidoscopic Lens: How Hollywood Views Ethnic Groups.* New York: Jerome S. Ozer, 1980.

> Contains a chapter on the Slavic stereotype in American film. Miller points out that there have been relatively few portrayals of Slavic Americans in American films. But a

A Polish American Photo Album

Baltic Sea

LITHUANIA

RUSSIA

• Gdansk

• Szczecin

• Poznan

• Warsaw

BELARUS

POLAND

• Lodz

GERMANY

• Krakow

CZECH REPUBLIC

SLOVAKIA

UKRAINE

Poland is surrounded by Russia, Lithuania, Belarus, Ukraine, Slovakia, the Czech Republic, and Germany. One might argue that it occupies one of Europe's most vulnerable locations. Throughout history the Poles have seen their nation's borders expand and contract as neighboring countries sought to control them. In fact, Poland ceased to exist as a country for more than 150 years. This tumultuous history has produced in the Poles a unique and fierce streak of independence, creativity, and resilience. From Poland's nineteenth-century freedom fighters to the brave, history-making vision of Lech Walesa, Poles have always demonstrated an ability to overcome incredible odds. Immigration to the United States provided a way for many Poles to transcend the poverty and political domination that characterized their lives in the late nineteenth and early twentieth centuries. Once in the United States, they applied their characteristic determination to the task of becoming Americans. They also immeasurably enriched the American cultural tapestry by continuing to embrace aspects of their Polish heritage. If you are of Polish descent, you share with many other Americans this long and noble past.

The exuberance and colorful costumes of Polish folk dancers are captured by the artist W.T. Benda (1873-1948) in this work, entitled *Polish Dance Krakowiak.*

A similarly festive and high-spirited dance is demonstrated by the Polish American Folk Dance Company at New York's Waldorf-Astoria Hotel. The company, based in Brooklyn, New York, wears authentic Polish-made costumes.

The city hall of Baltimore, Maryland, is decorated for the 1974 Summer Festival. The theme that year was "Sights and Sounds of Poland." Baltimore, a port city, received many of the early Polish immigrants, who in turn developed distinctly Polish American neighborhoods.

A Polish American Roman Catholic church is a picturesque element of the skyline of Adams, Massachusetts. In 1980, a study found that 76 percent of Polish American parishes were still active, serving an important social as well as religious function.

Gen. John Shalikashvili speaks at a press conference with President Bill Clinton in 1993, when
Shalikashvili was nominated to succeed Gen. Colin Powell as chair of the
Joint Chiefs of Staff. Shalikashvili, whose mother is Polish, was born in Poland.

Warsaw-born Zbigniew Brzezinski served as the National Security Advisor under President Jimmy Carter. Brzezinski is a historian and international political analyst.

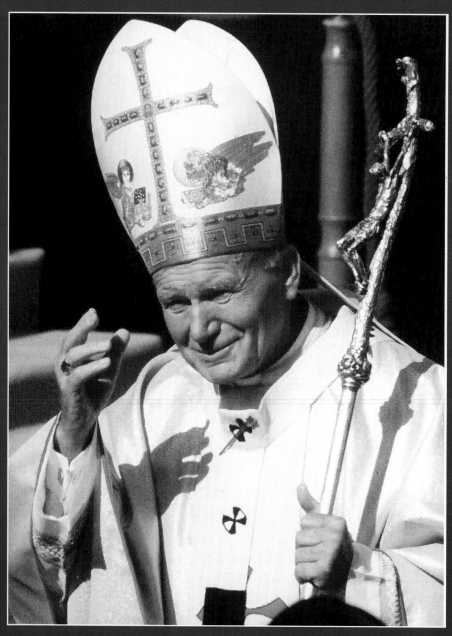

Karol Cardinal Wojtyla of Krakow became Pope John Paul II in 1978. His visit to Poland during the following year is believed to have been a factor in inspiring Poles to resist Communist rule. Above, the Pope waves to a crowd of faithful followers at Rome's Piazza Farnese in 1991.

Polish women turn out in national costume at the Jasna Gora Monastery in Czestochowa, Poland, during Pope John Paul II's 1979 homecoming.

The independent non-Communist labor union Solidarity began to make waves for Poland's Communist government in the 1980s. Solidarity was led by Lech Walesa, an electrician. Many Polish Americans and recent Polish émigrés supported the struggles of Solidarity. Above, a crowd in Warsaw raises the Solidarity banner outside Walesa's campaign headquarters in 1990.

Lech Walesa gives President George Bush the victory sign as First Lady Barbara Bush looks on. Walesa led the strikes of 1980 that preceded the formation of Solidarity. Arrested in 1981, he remained under government surveillance for the next several years. He was awarded the Nobel Peace Prize in 1983. Walesa had a major hand in replacing the Communist government with a Solidarity-led coalition in 1989, and in 1990 he was elected president of Poland.

Senator Barbara Mikulski, Democrat of Maryland, was first elected in 1986 and won a second term in 1992. She is a native of Baltimore. The great-granddaughter of Polish immigrants, Mikulski became the first woman to be elected to a leadership position in the Senate when she was elected Secretary of the Democratic Conference for the 104th Congress in 1994. She is also the first woman of the Democratic Party to serve in both houses of Congress, and the first woman to win a statewide election in Maryland.

stereotype has nevertheless been perpetuated, simplifying the characteristics of more than sixteen Slavic nationalities. In films, Slavs appear mainly as working-class, unskilled laborers.

Chapter 3
Beginning Your Genealogical Search

Before you begin your genealogical search, make sure of the most elementary facts. You may take your Polish American family name for granted, for example, but it is possible that it has been changed. Like other immigrants, Poles sometimes shortened their names or took new ones that were easier for English-speaking Americans to pronounce and spell. Thus Ludwik Sokolnicki, Carl Rollyson's grandfather, became Louis Sokolik. Polish names were often changed by immigration officials or employers, not necessarily by the individuals themselves.

If your Polish family came from parts of German- or Russian-occupied Poland, their names may reflect the influence of those languages. So ask your parents and grandparents and other relatives about the family name. Perhaps it has been modified as your family moved from Poland to the United States, or from one part of the United States to another. Several books on genealogy can help you start this process of verifying your family name and origins. Consult Gerald Ortell's book (listed in the **Resources** section of this chapter). He presents clear explanations of the evolution of Polish first and last names.

Getting Started

Now start with yourself. Take a sheet of $8^{1}/_{2} \times 11$-inch looseleaf paper. Write down your full name and date and place of birth. You can, of course, use a word processing program to record information. Be sure, however, to keep a hard (paper) copy set of files not only as backup (in case your computer files are destroyed), but as a sample you can show your family and other genealogical researchers. You might also want to write an autobiographical sketch, putting down what you have been told about the circumstances of your birth. List the *sources* of your information: parents, other relatives, neighbors, family friends. Be as specific as possible: Cite your sources by their full names, explaining their relationship to you, where they live (or lived), and anything else that might identify them. For example, if you have an older brother who tells you something about another relative, or about himself, make sure you identify him as your *source* and explain how he came by his information. It is easy to forget such details; writing them down will make a record that will come in handy when you interview your sources and learn things from other family members. More will be said about oral history interviews in the next chapter. For now, think of yourself as collecting information; interviewing will be the next stage of your genealogical search. Treat yourself as a *subject*. You are creating a *subject* file not only for yourself, but for other members of your family and for your descendants.

Make subject files of information about your brothers and sisters and parents. Make a file for each person. Put in photocopies of documents such as birth, marriage, and baptismal certificates. Perhaps you have an older brother who has been in the military service. Include photocopies of his discharge papers. Eventually you will find other documents—employment records, school report cards, award certificates, newspaper clippings with birth announcements and obituaries, announcements of engagements and marriages, photographs, burial records, and many other pieces of information that will eventually tell the story of your family.

Begin simply. Ask each member of your family to submit information for their subject file folder. Ask them also to specify their sources of information. Tell them that no detail is too trivial to record; it might help you to find other information. What seems insignificant to them may be a key piece of a family puzzle. Your family members may be too busy to write their own autobiographies, or they may initially seem uninterested in your family history. Be patient. Many of them will become involved in your search when they realize how serious and important it is. You will stimulate them to become enthusiastic participants by sharing your findings with them. They will also be impressed if they see you going about your search in an organized fashion.

It is important to standardize your records. Write or photocopy all information on the same size paper so that it can eventually be put into a looseleaf binder with dividers. It is preferable to photocopy any document a family member gives you. If you cannot afford photocopying or it is inconvenient, make sure you doublecheck the information you have copied from the originals. It is very easy to make errors.

Records and Documents

Genealogists do not consider anything to be "true" unless they have a record of it. Even though everyone in a family may agree on when a birth, marriage, or death occurred, you still need to obtain a copy of the paperwork that recorded the event. Records of births, deaths, and marriages are called vital records. To obtain copies of vital records for the United States, you need to know the county in which the event occurred. Then, contact the county courthouse by phone or letter. Tell them the person's full name, the event, and the date on which the event occurred. There may be a small fee for a copy of the document. The Government Printing Office can provide you with more information on finding vital records in its publication *Where to Write for Vital Records* (listed in the **Resources** section). Once you have the document, put it in the folder under the person's name.

Many Polish American families have traditionally been active in their local Catholic churches. The church should have records of christenings and other religious events that took place there. If you know the church your family attended, call or write them about accessing their records. Or, if your family is Jewish, your family synagogue may have records of events such as bar or bat mitzvahs that took place there.

Family history research may pique your interest in Poland's rich traditions and customs. You may learn about the traditional dress in the region your family hails from, for example. These Polish peasant women, pictured in 1936, came from Krobia, in South Poznan.

United States census records can be obtained from the National Archives in Washington, DC, one of its branches, large research libraries, or through the mail from the National Archives. You must know the name of the city or town where your ancestors lived and the year they lived there.

Before beginning your record-keeping and data collection, you might consult a book such as William Dollarhide's *Managing a Genealogical Project*. His book, described in the **Resources** section, gives examples of the forms and terms used by genealogists and family historians.

This chapter will describe many sources of information outside your own family, but it is essential that you begin in a simple and organized fashion. Be systematic so that you do not lose, misinterpret, or fail to make connections between different pieces of information. Each recorded fact may not seem important in itself, but it will ultimately contribute to an overall picture of your family.

After you have collected basic information about your immediate family, you need to decide how far back you wish to trace your roots: two, three, four generations? Polish Americans usually have parents, grandparents, or great-grandparents who immigrated to America. It will be quite a task to document three or four generations—yours, your parents, your grandparents, your great-grandparents. A typical genealogical search involves working back from the present to the point at which your ancestors emigrated from Poland to the United States. Of course, you may become interested in the history of your family in Poland beyond your grandparents' or great-grandparents' generation; but if you do, you should be prepared to conduct a lengthy search involving considerable correspondence and perhaps even travel to Poland.

Polish Records

Gerald Ortell's book, listed in **Resources**, will also be helpful if you are planning to trace your family's origins in Poland. He shows you how to read Polish parish records. Here again your family surname is crucial. Certain names are often associated with certain villages, Ortell points out. He even shows you how to distinguish between two villages or hamlets with the same name: Villages are listed at the top of a Polish parish's records. He also explains how to scan death registers for family names, and how to pick out the relevant information. Although you are probably not yet ready to investigate Polish records, Ortell's suggestions should be kept in mind. As you gather information about your Polish American family, you are also gleaning important information about your family's background in the old country that will prove invaluable if you later decide to investigate it. You may also wish to write to archives in Poland for copies of vital records. Requests to the State Archives must be made in Polish. There is an application fee and separate charges for documents and searches (by the hour). Write to Naczelna Dyrekcja Archiwow Panstwowych, ul. Dluga 6, skrytka pocztowa Nr 1005, 00-950 Warszawa, Polska. Reports in English require an additional charge. The United States Embassy in Warsaw may also be helpful in obtaining birth, marriage, and death records, but check first with the Polish Consulate in New York City, which can advise you on how to pursue your genealogical search. Call 212-779-3062.

The Mormon Church (The Church of Jesus Christ of Latter-day Saints) has microfilmed Polish archival records. Check to see if the church has a Family History Center near you. (The main address is listed in the **Resources** section). Church records are still held, however, by individual parishes in Poland.

How far you pursue your search may well depend on how much time you have and what you are willing to spend on research. The further you go back in time, the more likely it is that there will be gaps in your family tree and more branches of that tree you need to explore. Professional genealogists say that you cannot skip generations. Even if it is only your grandparents or great-grandparents that interest you, it would be a mistake to skip your parents' generation.

You must begin in the present, doing the proper ground-work; otherwise, you can easily make mistakes, misidentifying people and missing valuable information that appears as evidence only if you have approached it by working from the present to the past.

Before using libraries and other institutions, find out more about your family and about the places they lived and worked, making sure you have not overlooked evidence at home. Is there a family Bible? Does it record names, dates of birth, or perhaps other significant events in your family's history? Have family members kept scrapbooks, high school yearbooks, photographs? Do the photographs have names and dates on them? Perhaps your uncle or aunt—your father's or mother's brother or sister—also has such items. Often relatives have a family archive, but they do not think of their photograph albums and scrapbooks as historical evidence. This material may be in boxes somewhere in a basement or an attic. An old trunk could contain letters long forgotten. Offer to help relatives clean out drawers and cabinets. You might be surprised at what you find! People like to keep souvenirs of trips, vacations, military service, and so on. Even a postcard with a date stamp on it can lead to verifying a key event in family history or the whereabouts of relatives. Family members may say these things are only of "sentimental value," but to you they help establish not only facts but the character of your family.

When you have gathered all of your family's archive and organized it into subject files, think about your next step. Are you mainly interested in establishing a genealogy? Are you concerned, in other words, in simply tracing your roots and finding out whom you are related to, how many cousins you have, what parts of the country your family settled in, and so on? Or do you wish to write a family history, detailing some of the significant experiences of two, three, or four generations of Polish Americans? Writing a family history is a much more ambitious project than a genealogy; indeed, it could easily take up a good deal of your life or even become a lifelong project—if you keep your own diary or journal.

By proceeding step by step, beginning with yourself and working backward, you can maintain flexibility. Work first as a genealogist, and then see how much of a family historian you want to become. There may be members of the family who are willing to help you write your family history, or you may discover family members who know writers willing to become involved in your project. But you do not need to make such decisions until you've collected a significant body of material and done some interviewing. A later chapter provides specific advice on creating a family tree, writing an autobiography, a story, keeping a journal, a scrapbook, photohistory, or time capsule. There are many different ways of communicating what you have learned in your search. Think about which kind of project you would enjoy most, which one speaks to your strengths and interests, but also which one will help you learn the most about your Polish American roots.

When you have assembled everything in your family archive, the next step is to move outside the home. Do your parents or other family members belong to clubs, churches, labor unions, or other organizations that might keep records? A church might keep copies of newsletters with birth announcements or reports on the activities of its members. A club might have photograph albums or newspaper clipping files or trophy cases. Even if such sources do not yield specific information on your family, they will probably give you insight into the time in which your family lived and help to explain certain moves or decisions individual family members made when you see them as members of groups outside the home.

Libraries and Archives

Your first major step outside home and community archive building is library and public archive research. This may seem the daunting part of your search. Where to begin? Try your local library; it will have certain basic books about genealogical research and family history. Look under "genealogy" in the library's catalog. Do not forget to look for

Polish American trade union members demonstrate against the imposition of martial law in Poland in 1981. Many Polish Americans worked in industries with strong labor unions; union records may be helpful in your research.

books on oral history, autobiography, and diary and journal keeping. Check the catalog for books on these topics. These kinds of books will start you thinking about how you will compose and present your research to others. Remember also that libraries, even small ones, usually have bibliographies—listings of books on particular subjects. Sometimes the bibliographies are annotated, which means they give a brief description of each book that the bibliography lists.

Unless your local library is especially well equipped, the number of books you will find on genealogical research and family history will be limited, and the chances of your finding out specific information about your own family will be slim. Do not be discouraged. Try the main branch of your city or county library system. These larger libraries have considerable experience in dealing with genealogical searches. They often have brochures on the subject and staff members who can help you get started. You may also have access to computers that allow you to search for books and articles in other libraries, materials that can be obtained for you through interlibrary loan. Ask your school or public librarian about the Online Computer Library Center, Inc. (OCLC) online union catalog.

Below you will find a list of libraries, books, and organizations (such as genealogical societies) that will help you with your search. The resources in New York City and Washington, DC, are highlighted because so many records of immigrants are to be found in those two cities. But you do not need to travel to New York or Washington to conduct research. You can order material directly from sources. Several of the books listed below contain sections identifying libraries and other institutions throughout the country that serve genealogical searchers.

The sources listed below will introduce you to the value of many different kinds of evidence: deeds, mortgage papers, tax records, civil and criminal lawsuits filed in county courthouses, and census records (especially valuable for immigrants after 1900, listing full names, birthplaces, years of residence in the United States, occupation, and other details). These kinds of records will tell you both basic and more revealing information about your relatives.

As you will see, "how to" books on genealogical research and family history are plentiful. Almost any book can give you the basics. There are tried and true methods of research that you will see repeated in book after book. But because each researcher has tested his or her method through experience, there is something new to be gleaned from almost every source.

Each genealogical search and family history is, of course, unique. No book or article can guide you to exactly what you want to know. But that is part of the challenge and fun of tracing your roots. To avoid confusion, concentrate on a small number of general books on genealogy, explore their contents thoroughly, and make notes. Then gradually widen your reading, skimming books for aspects of searching that you need more information on.

Take, for example, Jeane Eddy Westin's book *Finding*

Your Roots (described in the **Resources** section). Note how she begins by discussing the origins of names. On page 18 she has a chart of occupational names and their translations. Thus "farmer" in Polish is *Kmiec* and "miner" is *Weglarz*. If your name has a specific meaning in Polish, it may be a clue to the origins of your family, leading you to the place or places from which your family emigrated. On page 26, Westin notes that your last name may have variant spellings, and she recommends trying out and speculating on every possible version.

Even if you do not locate the origins of a family name, you will undoubtedly learn a good deal about your family's history, and the search itself will reveal just how complex and fascinating a family's past can be.

The next step in Westin's book is her explanation of setting up a family history record. She gives examples of family questionnaires, a sample letter to a relative requesting information, and examples of family possessions that may yield valuable information. For example, a recipe or an embroidered cloth from a certain region of Poland may give you a clue to your ancestors' place of origin.

Westin then describes the Mormon genealogical library in Salt Lake City. This is a justly famous resource known to all genealogists. Westin explains how to use their microfilms (there are 220 branch libraries). She also describes some of the main branch public libraries that have genealogical departments. The public library in Fort Wayne, Indiana, the Free Library of Philadelphia, the New Orleans Public Library, the Los Angeles Public Library, and the New York City Public Library are mentioned, as well as genealogical societies and state libraries. Check your phone book for a local, state, or regional genealogical society; look under "Polish," too, in case there might be a local club or heritage society.

All these resources may seem overwhelming. But if you have already collected information from your family, you can begin to pinpoint which libraries and archives are likely to be of help to you. And never discount the help of local librarians. Even if they do not have the information themselves, they may be quite willing to think out loud with you. Never be afraid to ask the question, "If you were looking for such and such a record, where would you start?" Or "If your family came from—, where would you look for information?" The United States is full of amateur genealogists willing to swap stories about their quests for roots. Make your search as concrete and specific as you can, and information experts and buffs are likely to take an interest.

Plan time for excursions. For instance, on page 83, Westin describes cemetery visits, because gravestones can also provide vital information. Beyond what you might learn, however, is the sense of the past and of a different era that people often experience in visiting old graveyards. Take photos or make rubbings of family gravestones so you have a record of your visit.

As you read Westin's book, note how she progresses from the local and the immediate to the regional and the national. Thus it is no surprise that she does not deal with federal records until midway through her book. The structure of her approach emphasizes that genealogical searches are cumulative; one fact leads to another; facts begin to form a pattern—or rather, you start to see a pattern in the facts and your sense of family history expands.

Don't overlook the Internet as a rich source of genealogical information. If you have access to the Internet, search under terms such as "genealogy," "Poland," and "Polish Americans." You may find other genealogists willing to share information as well as names and addresses of genealogical libraries and societies.

The last stage in Westin's book is searching for records abroad. This may be your goal all along—to find exactly where your grandparents came from. But as Westin's book proves, to get to that goal demands a disciplined investigation of the present. You have to begin at home, now, in order to arrive at your family's home in Poland. The great poet T. S. Eliot put it well: "In my end is my beginning."

Resources

Several general reference works and journals will be helpful in your genealogical search. Only large public or research libraries are likely to have these publications. But ask your local or school librarian about obtaining the following items through interlibrary loan: *The Polish Genealogical Society Newsletter, Polish American Studies,* and *The Polish Review. The Polish Encyclopedia* (try to locate the 1972 reprint by Arno Press) contains much of the basic material used in *The Polish Genealogical Society Newsletter.*

Allen, Desmond Walls, and Billingsley, Carolyn Earle. *Beginner's Guide to Family History Research.* **Bountiful, UT: American Genealogical Lending Library, 1991.**

> A comprehensive introduction with chapters on home and family sources, organizing family records, using libraries and archives, census records, courthouse research, military records, ethnic genealogy, how to manage correspondence and queries, and adoptee searches for natural parents. Includes samples of how to record family data, a glossary, and a bibliography.

American Genealogical Lending Library
P.O. Box 244
Bountiful, UT 84010

> The library is part of an effort by the Mormons (The Church of Jesus Christ of Latter-day Saints) to compile repositories of genealogical records around the country. Check your local telephone directory or ask your librarian to find out if the Church has a Family History Center near

you. The library in Bountiful rents the use of census microfilm and has other rental programs that help with genealogical research. It has also developed a computer program, Personal Ancestry File, to manage genealogical research.

Ames, Mary Ann Boczon. *How to Research Your Personal Polish Family History.* **New Carrollton, MD: Mary Ann Boczon, 1976.**

Contains chapters on locating family roots in Poland, how to use archives, compiling a family history, and a bibliography. Boczon presents the format of a genogram, which is designed not merely to trace family relationships but to analyze the family's development over generations—whether it is increasing or decreasing, the ratio between males and females, and the educational and occupational backgrounds of several generations.

Chorzempa, Rosemary. *Korzenie Polskie Polish Roots.* **Baltimore: Genealogical Publishing Company, 1993.**

A comprehensive introduction to genealogical research. Chapter 1 describes how to search for funeral home records, cemetery and gravestone markers, obituaries, church records, fraternal societies, draft registration, consular records, and others. Chapter 2 gives names and addresses of libraries and archives; Chapter 3, Polish genealogical societies. Chapter 4 is a history of Poland and its social classes. Chapter 5 explains how to do research on different ethnic groups in Poland. Chapter 6 describes Poland's geographical regions; Chapter 7 explains how to use maps and gazetteers; Chapters 8 and 9 explain how to use religious records in Poland; Chapter 10 is devoted to civil records. Chapter 11 provides information on Polish surnames; Chapter 12 on Christian or first names. Chapter 13 is on the Polish language. Chapter 14 is a genealogical letter-writing guide. Chapter 15 contains advice on visiting Poland. Each chapter lists further resources, including many helpful addresses.

Dine, L. G. *The Genealogist's Encyclopedia.* **New York: Weybright and Talley, 1969.**

> Chapters on genealogy and the oral tradition, records in several European countries, heraldry, titles, a glossary of key terms and illustrations. References to Poland.

Directory of Archives and Manuscript Repositories in the United States. **Washington, DC: National Archives and Records Service, 1978.**

> Organized by state, a valuable list of addresses and phone numbers for libraries, historical societies, museums, and other repositories of manuscripts. A typical entry describes the repository's major holdings and cites other repositories that house similar material. Hours, terms of access (in some cases, special permission is required), and the availability of copying services are also noted.

Doane, Gilbert. *Searching for Your Ancestors: The How and Why of Genealogy.* **Minneapolis: University of Minnesota Press, 1960.**

> Chapters on family papers, town records, inscriptions in cemeteries, church records, government aid in research, and how to arrange a genealogy. Appendixes on bibliographies, locations of vital statistics, census records, and records dating to the Revolutionary War.

Dollarhide, William. *Managing a Genealogical Project.* **Baltimore: Genealogical Publishing Company, 1988.**

> Contains a list of sample forms (relationship chart, family data sheet, research log, ancestor table, research journal, correspondence log), types of genealogical projects and a glossary of genealogical relationships, collecting references (basic rules in note-taking), evaluating genealogical evidence, using a computer, and presentation techniques (pedigrees, biographies).

Family History Centers

For a list of locations, send a stamped, self-addressed envelope to:

**Family History Library
35 North West Temple Street
Salt Lake City, UT 84150**

Gateway to America: Genealogical Research in the New York State Library. **Albany: New York State Library, 1980.**

> A section on genealogical research in the state library and an introduction to searching and recording genealogical information or "forms for record." Also contains a helpful explanation of how genealogical works and records are organized, a listing of important books with their call numbers, floor diagrams of the library, a list of leading genealogical periodicals, and guides to local and state records.

Gnacinski, Jan, and Gnacinski, Len. *Polish and Proud: Tracing Your Polish Ancestry.* **West Allis, WI: Janlen Enterprises, 1979.**

> Chapters on emigration, vital statistics, census records, passenger arrival records, immigration and naturalization, military service records, city directories, libraries, ethnic newspapers, church records, periodicals, form letters (in Polish and English) for writing to Poland, an ancestor chart, and maps.

Greenwood, Val D. *The Researcher's Guide to American Genealogy.* **Baltimore: Genealogical Publishing Company, 1973.**

> A guide to genealogical basics. Several chapters on methods of research, kinds of records, using libraries and archives, interpreting data, writing letters of inquiry about genealogical research, and how to organize a "research calendar." Many samples of records are shown and explained.

Hanks, Patricia, and Hodges, Flavia. *A Dictionary of First Names.* **New York: Oxford University Press, 1990.**

> Look here to determine whether a relative's name, or even your own, is of Polish origin. An extensive survey of more

than 4,500 European and American names, giving the linguistic and ethnic root of each name, and usually the non-English form of the name. Diminutive (shortened) and pet names are also included.

————. *A Dictionary of Surnames*. **New York: Oxford University Press, 1989.**

An important source for genealogists and family historians, especially those searching for relatives whose names may have more than one national origin (e.g., Poles living in German-occupied Poland). A survey of the origins of 100,000 currently used surnames of European origin as they are found throughout the world.

Hey, David. *The Oxford Guide to Family History*. New York: Oxford University Press, 1993.

A guide to constructing a family tree, with an account of how families have functioned in history, chapters on researching court and municipal records and church registers, and the origins of family names.

Hoskins, Janina W. *Polish Genealogy and Heraldry: An Introduction to Research*. Washington, DC: Library of Congress, 1987.

Designed for both the historian and the family genealogical researcher, with sections on armorials and studies in heraldry, genealogy, English-language publications for Americans seeking their Polish heritage, bibliographies of source material, descriptions of encyclopedias, histories, geographic dictionaries, archives and printed sources, and other miscellaneous reference works. A section of useful addresses, including National Archives Field Branches in eleven major cities, and a chronology of Polish genealogy and heraldry.

Kemp, Thomas J. *Vital Records Handbook*. Baltimore: Genealogical Publishing Company, 1988.

Arranged alphabetically by state, addresses and phone

numbers for vital records, the cost of obtaining records such as birth, death, and marriage certificates, and copies of state forms requesting vital statistics. Separate section on Canadian provinces.

Konrad, J. *Polish Family Research*. Munroe Falls, OH: Summit Publications, 1992.

Chapters on Polish history, immigration, genealogical searches in the United States, and ancestor-hunting in Poland. Includes maps of Poland's partitions, its seventeen provinces before 1975, and the forty-nine provinces formed in 1975. Examples of ancestor charts (in Polish and English), family records, addresses and phone numbers of federal archive and record centers, how to access other records in each state, a list of Polish place names and their German equivalents (especially important if your ancestors emigrated from German-dominated Poland), selected Polish vocabulary, examples of Polish birth and death records, and a form letter in Polish to Polish sources.

Kurzweil, Arthur. *From Generation to Generation: How to Trace Your Jewish Genealogy and Personal History*. New York: William Morrow, 1980.

Chapters on why it is important to study genealogy, on beginning a genealogical search, and exploring records in the old country. Appendixes on a Jewish Family History. Workbook and readings on Jewish genealogy.

Kurzweil, Arthur, and Weiner, Miriam. *The Encyclopedia of Jewish Genealogy. Volume I: Sources in the United States and Canada*. Northvale, NJ: Jason Aronson, 1991.

Chapters on immigration and naturalization (federal court, passenger, and Ellis Island records), institutional records (arranged by city and state), appendixes on Jewish genealogical societies throughout the world, Jewish historical societies in North America, federal archives, and a listing of town plans in Poland.

National Archives
Northeast Division
201 Varick Street
New York, NY 10014
212-337-1300

Census records from 1790 to 1920, passenger arrivals, immigration and naturalization records, World War I draft records, federal court records.

National Archives and Records Administration
Washington, DC 20408

Request several free leaflets: *Military Services Records in the National Archives, Using Records in the National Archives for Genealogical Research,* and *Getting Started: Beginning Your Genealogical Research in the National Archives in Washington.*

National Genealogical Society
4527 17th Street North
Arlington, VA 22207

Request information on genealogical forms and research aids, family group sheet, and newsletter.

National Union Catalog of Manuscript Collections.

A multivolume series with supplements. Available in larger libraries, it lists holdings of manuscripts under individual surnames. This work may tell you if any members of your family have papers deposited in a library or archive in this country.

New York Genealogical and Biographical Society
122 East 58th Street
New York, NY 10022
212-755-8532

A source for land records, probate records, and surrogate court decisions. Includes materials on New England and the South.

Ortell, Gerald A. *Polish Parish Records of the Roman Catholic Church: Their Use and Understanding in Genealogical Research.* **Buffalo Grove, IL: Genun Publishers, 1989.**

Chapters on the evolution of parish records, farmers and serfdom, the spelling and structure of Polish names, Polish pronunciation, Polish given names (including Americanization of names), occupations, military references, and a chapter on methodologies, "Beginning the Search." Also includes chapters on and examples of marriage, baptismal, birth, and death records. Appendixes with a glossary of terms and a list of Polish Saints' Days. Readers of this book are encouraged to write the author with their questions, enclosing a stamped, self-addressed envelope: Gerald Ortell, 95-10 243rd Street, Bellerose Terrace, NY 11001.

Polish Genealogical Society of America
984 North Milwaukee Avenue
Chicago, Illinois 60622

Send a stamped, self-addressed envelope for their current list of publications.

Rottenberg, Dan. *Finding Our Fathers: A Guidebook to Jewish Genealogy.* **New York: Random House, 1977.**

Chapter 2, "Starting Out," has helpful examples of genealogical charts for beginners. Several excellent chapters on public records. See Chapter 7 for researching Jewish ancestry in Poland.

Rye, Walter. *Records and Record Searching*, **2d ed. Baltimore: Genealogical Publishing Company, 1969. [First published in 1897].**

Chapter 1 describes how to compile a pedigree; Chapters 3 and 4 cover land records and Chapters 8 and 9, church records.

Tepper, Michael. *American Passenger Records: A Guide to the Records of Immigrants Arriving at American Ports by Sail and Steam.* **Baltimore: Genealogical Publishing Company, 1993.**

> Contains information on records from the Colonial period to the beginning of mass immigration in the nineteenth and twentieth centuries. Several examples of passenger lists and how to read them. Appendix B contains titles of passenger list publications.

Wellauer, Maralyn A. *Tracing Your Polish Roots.* **Milwaukee, WI: Maralyn A. Wellauer, 1991.**

> A chapter on Poland's history and geography, sections on searching records of various kinds, including social security, alien registration, special Polish collections in American libraries, and genealogical societies. A chapter on locating towns in Poland, and bibliographies of writing on Polish Americans, of guide books to Polish genealogy, and sources of information in Poland.

Westin, Jeane Eddy. *Finding Your Roots: How Every American Can Trace His Ancestors—At Home and Abroad.* **New York: Ballantine Books, 1977.**

> Instructions on how to gather family records, using libraries and genealogical societies, local public records, and federal records. Discusses writing and publishing family history. Lists archives and stores specializing in genealogical searches.

Where to Write for Vital Records: Births, Deaths, Marriages and Divorces. **Superintendent of Documents, U.S. Government Printing Office, Washington, DC 20402.**

> This booklet provides valuable information on obtaining vital records.

Chapter 4
Oral History

Don't begin oral history interviews until you have amassed the documents and written statements concerning your family. Of course, in the process of gathering information, you may already have had conversations with family members. This is natural, and you should make notes of these talks. But also let family members know that you will be talking with them again as soon as you have had a chance to assemble all your material and formulate some questions. Tell family members that your research will be done in several stages and that you may have to speak with them several times. Let them know that they are part of a process; they will be more likely to be cooperative when they realize that you have a plan and an organized method of research.

There is nothing wrong with being informal—indeed, don't make family members feel they are being studied, but rather that they are an integral part of a family history and that what you are doing for yourself is also being done for them. Prepare them for the next stage: an interview that requires concentration and preparation.

Plan for the interview by developing a set of questions. Make the first questions as open-ended as possible: "What do you remember about . . . ?" Gradually make the questions more specific. Think about the order of the questions. Start with fairly simple ones; save complicated issues for later. Do not force your interviewee to struggle for answers right at the beginning of the interview. You want him or her to feel comfortable and confident.

You will want to begin by asking a sequence of questions, starting with factual ones about age, place of birth, ethnic origin, occupation, religion, and politics. Then move on to

If your interviewee lived in a largely Polish American community, you might ask about local institutions, such as churches, that brought the community together. This 1939 photo shows Polish Americans in prayer on the steps of Pittsburgh's Polish community church after news of the bombing of Warsaw was received.

questions about family history—the birthplace of your interviewee's parents, their occupations, all of their household members; if immigrants, why and when they settled in the United States, the other places they lived, port of entry, and so on. Your questions should gradually move backward in time, taking the interviewee from data he or she is likely to know well and gradually delving into the more distant past.

Then ask your interviewee about his or her occupational history (starting this time with his or her earliest job, so that you have a sense of a developing biography). Move on to questions about schooling, travels, experiences with other ethnic groups, and political activity. Then move to questions about family relations—your interviewee's relationship with his or her mother and father. Ask straightforward questions. Were your parents strict? Did they work away from home a great deal? Did they remain in Polish American neighborhoods? How did each parent feel about education? What differences do you see between your parents' attitudes and yours?

Ask your interviewees to bring to the interview any written information that might help you. Half the fun of interviews comes from relatives who have photographs to show or other prized possessions to share. A relative might produce an award, a trophy, a badge—anything that has a story.

Conduct the interview in a quiet place away from distractions. The interview should not be interrupted; privacy will make the interviewee less self-conscious.

Ask your interviewee if you may use a tape recorder. Use a small, unobtrusive recorder with a built-in microphone. Do not rush the interview—sometimes the best information is obtained after you turn the tape recorder off. If you think the recorder will make your interviewee uncomfortable, talk for a few minutes with it off, and then casually ask if it can be turned on. Even if you are refused, you might find another point in the interview when you might say, "Your words are so important, would you mind if I record this part of the interview?"

In an interview, you might ask questions about your interviewee's political beliefs and affiliations, and whether they are influenced by his or her Polish heritage. Here a group of Polish Americans express their support for Senator Edmund Muskie in his campaign for the presidential nomination in 1972.

Carl Rollyson has interviewed hundreds of people for biographies he has written of notable public figures. He often finds the most trouble with people who have been interviewed several times or feel that they do not have much to say. He has discovered that talking about himself, about his interest in the subject and his hopes for his project, elicits people's sympathy and interest. He tells them he wants to hear about their impressions—not just facts. He also offers to show them the results of the interview, saying that they are free to correct misstatements and grammatical errors. This shared activity has often led interviewees to supply much more information than they thought they had; writer Dashiell Hammett's daughter, for example, produced a shoebox stuffed with valuable letters. At first she had been unwilling to have her voice tape recorded; yet later in the same interview she offered not only to read the letters into the recorder but to comment on them, thus giving valuable background information and setting the letters in their historical context.

Carl also got spectacular results with his eighty-five-year-old Polish grandfather. One day he sat his grandfather down in front of a tape recorder and played back a small excerpt of Carl's telling a joke. At the punchline Carl's mother, sister, and grandmother laughed. Immediately, Carl's grandfather took over the microphone (this was years before the small recorders with built-in microphones were available) and began to tell jokes that were more than sixty years old—having to do with life on Polish farms, horse-trading, and peasant life. The family were enthralled and amazed. Carl's grandfather probably hadn't thought about this past life for years. Somehow, turning on the tape recorder also turned on a fountain of memory.

Interviewing Tips

Some people feel uneasy or embarrassed having their voices recorded. This may be the case if you are interviewing a close relative. Explain why you are using the tape recorder. Also take notes, which will serve as a backup should your recorder develop mechanical problems. Note-taking helps you to concentrate. With the machine recording what your interviewee is saying, you will be freer to make your own comments in writing, or you may have a chance to write down questions that did not occur to you beforehand.

Notetaking is also a kind of "cover" for both you and your interviewee. Without meaning to, you might ask an embarrassing question. You can "cover" the embarrassment by looking down at your notebook, not at him or her. Difficult questions take time to answer. The interviewee may hesitate, feel awkward, and want to give up answering or avoid the question. Rephrase the question, make notes to yourself, filling in an awkward silence with the sound of your pen writing in your notebook.

Allow the interviewee to settle into a relaxed rhythm. Don't force questions. Don't ask too many questions at once. Above all, don't cut off the interviewee because you have something interesting to say. Instead, make a note of what you want to say and say it later when there is a lull in the conversation. There may be interviews in which you have to "prime the pump"—that is, get the interviewee interested and excited by telling him or her some things you have already learned. The interviewee may then catch your enthusiasm and open up.

If you are having difficulty with an interview, make notes to yourself about why you think there is a problem. If you keep yourself busy writing, your interviewee may feel compelled to say more to fill up the silence. Sometimes you can also lead a reluctant interviewee by asking, "Is there anything you want to ask me?" Or you might say a little about your other interviewees and what you have learned. Sometimes people are waiting for the interviewer to tell them something new, or they are wondering just how much the interviewer knows. Once they are assured that the interviewer has done his or her homework, they are willing to contribute to a valuable project.

The foregoing advice may make interviewing seem terribly complex and fraught with difficulties. In fact, most interviews are pleasant and stimulating experiences. Interviewees often come out of them saying they never realized they knew so much or that being interviewed could be so much fun. The interview may stimulate them to look for new information.

You will find after doing a few interviews that the psychology of interviewing can be mastered and that much of it is quite natural; it is what people do all the time in less formal contexts. Interviewing is simply a matter of cultivating social skills you already possess. You are sizing up a situation and deciding when to be tactful, when to be direct, when to push a point, when to back off. It may help to speak your interviewee's language. You may not speak Polish, but using certain Polish words in the interview or asking for the Polish equivalents of certain English words and writing them down might also impress your interviewee. After a successful interview, both people feel that they have learned something.

Above all, respect the interviewee's way of doing things. Some people need a long time to warm up; other people want to plunge right in and you will have difficulty stopping their talk or getting all your questions answered. Let them talk. Do not worry about digressions or get upset because the interviewee seems to have wandered from the point. This is a natural part of talking. Don't cut off the interviewee's stories, even if they seem irrelevant. Find a moment when you can redirect his or her attention by asking another question. What seems irrelevant during the time of an interview may become surprisingly apt when you review the tape or type a transcript of it.

You will sometimes end an interview thinking you have learned very little. Don't be so sure. Listen to the tape. Sometimes a comment or opinion may lead toward certain facts. Sometimes you find that you missed a clue the interviewee was giving you. This is not surprising, and you should not be reluctant to reinterview your subject. In some cases, perhaps a telephone call or casual conversation will be enough to secure what you need. For reasons of health or age, some people do not want to be taxed with long interviews; often short bursts on the phone or in person get the best results. Always let the interviewees know that you may have more questions for them, and thank them for being so generous with their time. Follow up with a thank-you letter. Don't forget to ask them if they have found any new documents, papers, or pictures for you. Always write up a record of any conversation, no matter how brief. It is best to do this immediately while the details are fresh in your mind.

It can be quite time-consuming to type transcripts of oral history tapes. Perhaps there are members of the family who can help you. If not, consider indexing your tape recordings. Use a tape recorder with a counter and make a subject and name index. For example:

009 Uncle Stanislaw's first memories of his New York City neighborhood; 146 Uncle Stanislaw's version of why grandfather left the old country.

Polish parish records may contain records of your ancestors' marriages. Here, Polish newlyweds leave the church wearing traditional wedding costumes after a ceremony in Zakopane, Poland, in 1936.

By indexing tapes you can avoid the repetitious parts and the digressions and replay just those passages that interest you and that you may want to write up as part of your family history.

Interviewing Through the Mail

Writing letters may also be an option. It is said that most people do not write letters today, but some of the older members of your family might enjoy corresponding with you, especially if they live far away. Telephone calls can be expensive. If you write short letters asking a few pertinent questions, they may be willing to reply. Their replies may give you an opening to send another letter with a few more questions. Even if your letters are not answered, you can then call your relatives or family friends, knowing that your letters have given them a chance to think of a response to your call.

After Carl's father died, Carl began a correspondence with one of his father's brothers. He had questions about what it was like for his father and his family growing up in West Virginia. Carl's Uncle Hoy, approaching his middle seventies, was eager to talk about it, especially since Hoy had found it difficult to communicate with his own son. Soon Hoy was sending Carl several pages of reminiscences. When Hoy died a few years later, Carl read parts of these letters to family and friends at a memorial service. The family was stunned. Hoy had been such a quiet, reserved man. No one realized that he had such a reservoir of passionate memories about his life.

If you have access to electronic mail (e-mail), you may actually be able to form a circle of correspondents willing to handle your questions and provide advice or information. Several computer services, such as CompuServe, now have e-mail, a way to communicate through a telephone modem attached to a computer. You can often get a busy person's attention if you make contact via a modem rather than a telephone or mailed letter. This new form of communication will add an immediacy and excitement to your search that other relatives might want to share.

Resources

Allen, Barbara, and Montell, William Lynwood. *From Memory to History: Using Oral Sources in Local Historical Research.* **Nashville, TN: American Association for State and Local History, 1981.**

> Particularly stimulating reading for researchers who have assembled an archive of oral histories and wish to write a family or public history based on the material. See Chapter 6: "Producing a Manuscript from Oral Sources."

Bodnar, John. *Workers' World: Kinship, Community, and Protest in an Industrial Society, 1840–1940.* **Baltimore: Johns Hopkins University Press, 1982.**

> An excellent collection of oral history interviews with Polish Americans, many of them second generation, involved in coal mining and steelmaking. They provide remarkable insights into working-class culture in early twentieth-century Pennsylvania.

Bremmer, Robert H., ed. *Essays on History and Literature.* **Columbus: Ohio State University Press, 1966.**

> Daniel Aaron's essay "The Treachery of Recollection: The Inner and the Outer History" is an informative discussion of how historians treat contemporary history and living memory.

Davis, Cullom; Back, Kathryn; and Maclean; Kay. *Oral History: From Tape to Type.* **Chicago: American Library Association, 1977.**

Chapters on collecting oral history, interviewing, transcribing, and editing. Contains a glossary, a bibliography, and several illustrations of how to organize interviews, do cross-referencing, and take notes.

Deering, Mary Jo, and Pomeroy, Barbara. *Transcribing Without Tears: A Guide to Transcribing and Editing Oral History Interviews.* **Washington, DC: Oral History Program, George Washington University Library, 1976.**

How to deal with problems such as overlapping speech, syntax, inaccuracies, false starts, dangling sentences, fuzzy thinking, and paragraphing. How to use editing symbols such as ellipses, dashes, brackets, and footnotes.

Degh, Linda; Glassie, Henry; and Oinas, Felix J., eds. *Folklore Today.* **Bloomington: Indiana University Press, 1976.**

In "Legend: Oral Tradition in the Modern Experience," William Hugh Janson provides insights into how oral narratives are constructed by both those telling the story and those listening to it. Although this is an article meant for scholars, it is worth studying because it reveals how families and other groups shape their history.

Evans, George Ewart. *Spoken History.* **London: Faber & Faber, 1987.**

In the chapter "The Interview," Evans discusses what it is like to interview people not accustomed to tape recorders.

Garner, Van Hastings. *Oral History: A New Experience in Learning.* **Dayton, OH: Pflaum Publishing, 1975.**

Chapters on equipment, how to set up interviews, organization of the interview, technique, and style. Contains a bibliography.

Harris, Ramon, et al. *The Practice of Oral History.* **Glen Rock, NJ: Microfilming Corporation of America, 1975.**

Chapters on preparing for interviews, processing and editing interviews, present and future uses of oral history. Appendixes: helpful hints for interviewers, samples of log book form, and other archival forms.

Hoopes, James. *Oral History: An Introduction for Students*. Chapel Hill: University of North Carolina Press, 1979.

Chapters on arranging, preparing, conducting interviews, and on how to then use interview material for papers. A listing of oral history collections and sources. Contains a bibliography.

Ives, Edward I. *The Tape-Recorded Interview: A Manual for Field Workers in Folklore and Oral History*. Knoxville: University of Tennessee Press, 1974.

Chapters on tape recorders and their functions, interviewing techniques, and how to make a transcript of the interview. The appendix includes a compendium of forms used by the Northeast Archives of Folklore and Oral History. Also included are illustrations of edited oral history transcripts, letters to interviewees, and release forms (used for getting permission to use interviewees' remarks). Includes a brief bibliography.

Jorgensen, Danny L. *Participant Observation: A Methodology for Human Studies*. Newbury Park, CA: Sage Publications, 1989.

Chapters 6, 7, and 8 discuss interviewing, record-keeping, and ways of reconstructing what you learn from your interviews and observations. Contains a bibliography.

Meckler, Alan M., and McMullin, Ruth. *Oral History Collections*. New York: R. R. Bowker, 1975.

Divided into name and subject indexes. Listings for individuals, states, and organizations. Separate sections on U.S. and Foreign Oral History Centers.

Schumacher, Michael. *Creative Conversations: The Writer's Complete Guide to Conducting Interviews.* **Cincinnati: Writer's Digest Books, 1990.**

See especially the first chapter, "The Interview and Its Uses." Although this is a book for professional writers, it contains many useful tips for the family historian and genealogist.

Terkel, Studs. *Hard Times: An Oral History of the Depression.* **New York: Avon Books, 1971.**

A popular oral historian, Terkel provides a good model of how to shape and organize your oral history interviews. Pay close attention to the way he structures his book, emphasizing the themes that arise out of his interviewees' recollections.

Thompson, Paul. *The Voice of the Past: Oral History.* **New York: Oxford University Press, 1978.**

Explores the method and meaning of oral history. The chapter on "The Interview" gives tips on sequencing and phrasing questions and how to handle a tape recorder so as to actually increase the amount of information people give you. Sections on further reading, notes, and model questions for the oral history interview.

Tonkin, Elizabeth. *Narrating Our Pasts: The Social Construction of Oral History.* **Cambridge: Cambridge University Press, 1992.**

A difficult book for advanced readers interested in the questions oral history raises: how truthful are oral accounts of the past, and to what extent can we rely on autobiographies? Contains a bibliography.

Vansina, Jan. *Oral Tradition as History.* **Madison: University of Wisconsin Press, 1985.**

For advanced readers wishing to explore how to interpret oral histories. Even beginners, however, will profit from the first chapter's discussion of the different kinds of evidence to be found in oral history interviews and the oral tradition. The last chapter assesses the strengths and limitations of the oral tradition.

Chapter 5
Creating a Family Tree

With the basic genealogical information from various papers and oral history interviews in hand, you are ready to fashion a family tree. This will be a record of family relationships that will prove tremendously helpful in writing a family history (discussed in the next chapter). You may want to begin putting together a family tree even before you have all of the information in hand; it will provide an organizing principle for genealogical research. There may be gaps in the tree, but these can be filled in with further research—or perhaps left for another researcher in your family, if you have exhausted your time for the project or have not been able to recover some of the data.

Begin assembling the tree by concentrating on the family member from whom you trace your family's Polish American roots, your Polish American progenitor. Write a paragraph giving that individual's dates of birth and death, parentage (if known), and your sources of information. Then start another paragraph, specifying his or her date and place of marriage (or give approximate dates and the sources on which you base your statement). Give the spouse's full name and parentage, as well as the dates of the spouse's birth and death. List other facts that reveal his or her origins and life history: Was there a previous marriage? To whom? Were there children from the previous marriage? Do you know their names? If your progenitor was married several times, write a separate paragraph on the facts of each marriage.

Remember that in your initial paragraphs you are recording facts. Save interesting and colorful details for the next part of your family tree. It is important to establish as clearly as possible what you know about your progenitor and spouse and how you know it. Other family members may be able to add to or correct this record once they see it set down; your account may prove helpful to a later family historian.

With the facts clearly established, write an account of your progenitor's life. If you know anything about his or her place of birth or first memories, begin by recording them. Then state what you know about his or her schooling, military service, jobs or offices held, travels—all the details that will fill out a picture of a life. Include reminiscences about him or her that you obtained in oral history interviews or in letters. If your progenitor left a will, it may also say something about the kind of person he or she was, and you may want to comment on it.

If you have your progenitor's will, pay close attention to how children are mentioned. Summarizing the provisions made for them may be a good way to introduce their place in the family. Give each of them at least a paragraph or two. As you add paragraphs, you will be providing a picture of a generation—perhaps the first family generation that reached the United States. If so, think of adding material about Poland and about immigration to this country from the history and literature books you have read. You may begin to see how your family fit into the great movement of people to a new land. If you do refer to material you have read, be certain to specify your sources—the author, title, publisher, and date of the work you have relied upon.

There are several models you can consult in creating a family tree. You can follow an outline form, create a chart of family relationships, or design a diagram that shows how different branches of the family split off from your progenitor. For examples of family trees, consult the **Resources** section of this chapter.

Think of the family tree as your family's skeleton. It sets out the basic relationships. It also maps your family's movements. The family tree is the foundation on which you can erect a full family history. The next chapter provides several examples of what might be called family history extensions of the family tree. What you make of the tree depends greatly on your personality and interests. It may serve as the basis of your autobiography. It may introduce a family scrapbook of reminiscences and documents. It could serve to clarify relationships for readers of your family's oral history.

The family tree is both a starting and ending point. Do not be discouraged if there are gaps in the tree. Other family members may eventually discover new information—literally digging it up out of old trunks and boxes of papers long forgotten. The tree itself establishes the importance of your family history and may well stimulate family discussion that will contribute additional data.

Genograms

After reading Chapter 7 on the meaning of kinship, consider constructing what Monica McGoldrick and Randy Gerson call a genogram of your family (see **Resources** section). This is not merely a chart or diagram of family bloodlines, but a way of tracing the psychological patterns of interaction in a family. Family therapists and physicians have used genograms in treating patients, but McGoldrick and Gerson present a persuasive case for genograms as a tool for understanding family history that should be available to a wider audience. They stress that there is no one way to make a genogram; what it looks like depends very much on your family history and your understanding of kinship patterns. But you can learn a standardized format for the genogram and adapt it to your specific concerns. For example, you may become particularly interested in the gender relationships in your family, how men and women, mothers and fathers, have interacted over three generations (the minimum number recommended for genograms). Males can be designated by a square, females by a circle. For a person who is dead, an × can be put inside the square or circle. The years the person was born and died can be put to the left or right of the figure. Thus 19 [×] 62 represents a male who was born in 1919 and died in 1962. A triangle can represent a pregnancy. Still other symbols for stillbirths, spontaneous or induced abortions, separations and divorces, and other events in the lives of families and individuals can be incorporated into the genogram.

The genogram is a kind of psychological history of a family. It can help pinpoint recurrent patterns in family relationships. Studying the birth order in your family (sons first or daughters?) may also say something about how your family planned and organized itself. Putting family information in the form of a genogram will sharpen your understanding of closeness and distance between family members and whether patterns of behavior or certain events (divorces, adoptions, and so on) persist over several generations. As McGoldrick and Gerson point out, families often develop subsystems— particularly strong bonds between certain family members. Often these subsystems are triangles, coalitions that remain stable over several generations.

Genograms are a way of "mapping the family structure," McGoldrick and Gerson suggest, a graphic representation of family life. Their book presents genograms for unmarried couples, families with foster children, a woman with several husbands, and various other situations. They construct genograms for famous individuals such as Sigmund Freud and for families in works of literature, such as the Tyrone family in Eugene O'Neill's play *Long Day's Journey into Night*. They even have genograms that picture the pattern or route of the family history you have been tracing, allowing room for recording discrepancies in your data or conflicts between your sources of information.

McGoldrick and Gerson provide sections on how to conduct a genogram interview, the best way to pose sensitive questions about serious problems, work history, drugs and alcohol, and trouble with the law. You may not wish to pursue all of their suggestions; indeed, your family history may not require you to explore all of the issues that genograms are equipped to picture. But the concept of the genogram will stimulate you to think about the best way to organize your family history and to decide where you wish to put your emphasis.

Resources

Gouldrup, Lawrence P. *Writing the Family Narrative*. Salt Lake City: Ancestry, Inc., 1993.

A guide specifically for family history writers. Gouldrup provides suggestions on what kinds of information to include as well as style tips.

McGoldrick, Monica, and Gerson, Randy. *Genograms in Family Assessment*. New York: W. W. Norton, 1985.

After studying some of the genogram examples, see Chapter 3, "Interpreting Genograms," which shows different models for portraying family structure and households, sibling constellations, birth order, the concept of the life cycle and the transitions families go through, patterns of functioning and relationships, the impacts of various life events, social, economic, and political events, relational patterns and triangles, multigenerational triangles, relationships outside the family, role-playing, and level and style of functioning.

**National Genealogical Society
4527 17th Street North
Arlington, VA 22207-0363**

Request information on their genealogical forms and research aids, their family group sheet, and newsletter.

Polking, Kirk. *Writing Family Histories and Memoirs*. Cincinnati: Writer's Digest Press, 1995.

Chapters on how to begin writing a family history (involving your family, getting help from others, learning how to write dialogue), ideas for topics, becoming the family historian, where to find things in libraries, courthouses, electronic search services, tips on interviewing, different methods of organization, format and writing style, and editing and publishing a manuscript. Contains a bibliography.

Shull, Wilma Sadler. *Photographing Your Heritage.* **Salt Lake City: Ancestry, 1989.**

You might consider illustrating your family tree with photographs. This book provides tips on how to take effective photographs of relatives, family heirlooms, houses, and other things important to your family history.

Zinsser, William. *On Writing Well: An Informal Guide to Writing Nonfiction.* **New York: Harper & Row, 1985.**

Consult this book for general tips that can help to make your family history readable and interesting.

Chapter 6
Making a Polish American Family History

There are many ways to write the history of a family. One form of personal and familial history is the autobiography. See the **Resources** sections at the end of this chapter and Chapter 2 for examples of autobiography and journal writing. Autobiography is an attractive form because you can suit it exactly to your personality.

Some autobiographies are straightforward and chronological. They aim to give readers an exact, historical accounting of a life. But even here there are choices to make. Which generation do you begin with? Your great-grandparents? Your grandparents? Or do you want to reverse the chronology, beginning with yourself in the present and the reasons for your interest in family history? Perhaps some incident has stimulated your interest in genealogy. Or perhaps there is an event in your family's past that sums up your own need to learn about your Polish roots. Or you might begin with something that one of your interviewees said.

Some autobiographies are not chronological. They take the form of snapshots or glimpses of the past. You might want to begin with what you know about your family and then speak of the gaps in your evidence of what you do not know. You might want to speculate, mentioning family members who have fascinated you but who may still seem elusive and hard to know. In other words, you can write about the *process* of searching for your roots, not just about the results of your investigation.

Family history can be a kind of scrapbook, in which you surround pictures, documents, and other papers with your commentary. Where information is missing, you might ask questions. Who knows? Perhaps someone else in your family will follow in your footsteps and learn more of the family history than you were able to discover.

Does your family have an oral tradition? Does it have stories told over and over again? Do different members of the family tell the stories differently? Can you sort through this material and provide a complete account of the different stories? Or can you provide a narrative of different accounts? Some aspects of the oral tradition may be confirmed or refuted by the records you find. The differences between the oral and written record might well be a part of your family history, showing how each family member has adapted that history to his or her own personality. Perhaps you can find an event that several members of the family witnessed or heard about. Compare their different versions of the event. Are there neighbors or others outside the family who might be able to provide perspectives?

Consider the role of family gossip. All families, friends, groups, and communities gossip. Published biographies often contain a considerable amount of gossip. What role has gossip played in your family? Has it served to distort facts? Or is gossip sometimes helpful, allowing people to get used to certain events and experiences? Think about the difference between eyewitnesses, hearsay, reminiscences, dreams, and commentaries as evidence in family history. To what extent is your family's understanding of itself a social construction, an agreed upon set of anecdotes and values, and how much of it is factually true? See the **Resources** section of Chapter 4 for readings that will help you consider the meaning of oral history and oral traditions.

Another possibility is to tell your family history through memoirs. Here your oral history tapes will be most helpful. You may want to transcribe and edit certain sections, adding your own commentary, introduction, and conclusion, and asking other family members to contribute their thoughts as well. The result will be a unique family album of experience.

Additional topics: Explore anecdotes about the old country, about the trip to the United States and the first days here. What about the first jobs of your Polish American

Asking your relatives about jobs they or their parents have held may yield interesting stories. Many Polish immigrants to the United States performed backbreaking labor in mines and factories. This 1940 photo depicts the family of a Polish immigrant working as a miner in Pennsylvania.

ancestors? Where did they first live? How do the surviving members of the immigrant generation feel now about leaving the old country? Did they return to Poland after coming to the United States? Some of your best material may come from memories contrasting life here and there.

Perhaps there is a member of the family that you most admire and whose experience symbolizes your Polish American heritage. You might organize your history around him or her, using excerpts from an interview and reminiscences from other family members, as well as various documents, papers, and photographs. In effect, your history would become a biography, but one that says much about your interests and those of your family.

No matter what form family history takes—a journal, an autobiography, a biography, an oral history, an album, a scrapbook—your account will have much in common with the dynamics of family life that researchers have been studying for generations. You might find it useful to consult some of the books based on this research; studying the concept of the family may well provide you with a perspective on your own experience, a way to "place" the way family members behave in the continuum and the conflicts of family life. Chapter 7 on Your Kin Group or Family may help you sort through what could be both an exhilarating and troubling experience. It is possible that you may uncover family secrets. Such secrets, tacitly passed on from one generation to the next, may also be part of the folklore of family life. This folklore may well help you to define your own family's history.

Several books on the Polish family are described at the end of this chapter, as well as in Chapter 7. They will give you considerable perspective on your own family's history as you read about other families from a cross-cultural perspective, studying how the children in other immigrant groups have coped with the process of assimilation.

In multiethnic America, it has always been an open question how much an immigrant group must absorb of the prevailing culture. Should the children of immigrants retain

Poles in Poland are proud of the many Polish Americans who have distinguished themselves, such as Carl Yastrzemski, a star Red Sox outfielder in the 1960s.

their parents' language? Should that language be taught in school? How has your family reacted to these questions? Has it consciously tried to preserve its Polish roots? Or has it conformed with the tradition of the "melting pot" in which immigrants from different countries are envisioned as forming a new ethnic group of Americans, as described in Crevecoeur's *Letters of an American Farmer* (**Resources**, Chapter 1).

Inevitably, raising such questions will tell you something about your family's reaction to becoming American, and the story of what the United States means will become a part of your family history. The oral history by Studs Terkel (**Resources**, Chapter 4) may be helpful in putting your family into the context of the United States' other immigrant families. The autobiography of Alfred Kazin will also help you to focus on the uniqueness of your own family's experience.

Telling Your Story

As noted in the **Resources** sections, several Polish American writers have turned to fiction as a means of relaying family history. Fiction is often grounded in fact, but the novelist or short story writer feels free to elaborate on characters and events in ways not open to historians and biographers. Do not reject fiction as merely being untrue. Often it can convey feelings more powerfully than factual narrative, allowing you to fill in the gaps of your family tree, and to imagine the experiences of your progenitors even though you do not have enough information about them for a conventional history.

In telling your family's history, do not overlook the new technology of storytelling. Old photographs and super 8 films can be transferred to videotape; you may also wish to videotape some of your interviews and edit a kind of visual scrapbook or documentary. Desktop publishing computer software programs allow you to assemble at home a very neat, professional book of your own history.

Whatever approach you take toward family history, it will reveal that what it means to be an immigrant, and more specifically a Polish American, has changed from one generation to the next. Even within a generation, you may find that attitudes changed over the years as, say, your grandmother and grandfather responded to their experience in this country.

Visiting Poland

At some point, you may wish to travel to Poland—not merely to trace your roots, but also to encounter what might be called your "parent culture," the birthplace of your family's progenitors. You will encounter there a very rich tradition of story and legend about the United States. Poles are very proud of their Polish American relatives. They have always regarded the United States as a land of promise, where freedom reigns. Indeed, you may find that some of them have an exaggerated idea of American wealth and power. At the same time, Poland has gone through momentous changes, and its popular culture has been immensely influenced by the United States.

Prepare yourself for a Polish trip by reading works about the country's history and culture listed in the **Resources** section of Chapter 2. There you will also find works of fiction, poetry, and drama, revealing that in spite of its catastrophic history, Poland has maintained a rich literary and artistic tradition—one that Polish Americans have not always acknowledged or studied, often because they have assimilated American ideas and values so sincerely and rapidly. By mastering some portion of Polish writing, you will not only be learning from a great body of literature, but also constructing yet another perspective on your family's journey from the old country to the new.

As you read about Polish politics, about the Solidarity movement in Poland that eventually led to the fall of the country's Communist government, you will be confronting the issues of self-determination and democracy that Polish Americans have striven for in this country. Even if your family has had no direct involvement in politics, you will probably find that it does have certain convictions, a kind of philosophy, about the roles of the individual and the state.

Polish Americans in Chicago voice their disapproval of the actions of Poland's Communist government in 1981.

They will have strong feelings about the Polish past—Russia's domination of Poland, for example. In subtle ways, their feelings will have influenced what they think about contemporary politics, about the place of the United States in the world.

Tracing your Polish American roots, then, will involve you in a quest. Think of it as a kind of detective story. You are not only uncovering facts, you are laying bare attitudes, recovering and verifying memories, perhaps reuniting family members or strengthening your family's sense of their own experience, finding your own branch of the family tree, exploring how different generations have contributed to that branch, providing a record for future generations, and enriching what it means to be a Polish American.

Resources

AUTOBIOGRAPHY   (See also the section on Polish American autobiographies in Chapter 1 **Resources**)

Kazin, Alfred. *A Walker in the City*. New York: Harcourt, Brace and Company.

> Reprinted many times in paperback. A classic account of literary critic Alfred Kazin's growing up in a Jewish immigrant family in east Brooklyn, New York.

Padover, Saul K., ed. *Confessions and Self-Portraits: 4600 Years of Autobiography*. New York: John Day Company, 1957.

> A comprehensive selection of authors that displays the many different forms of autobiography. Writing an autobiography is an excellent way to record the daily events in the lives of you and your family.

Progoff, Ira. *At a Journal Workshop: The Basic Text and Guide for Using the Intensive Journal*. New York: Dialogue House, 1975.

> Progoff has run journal workshops all over the country. He has pioneered the use of journal writing for a complex of purposes: for personal growth, as a prelude to other kinds of writing (including fiction, history, autobiography). This book suggests many different ways of keeping journals, of writing about dreams, of tracking various periods in our lives, of keeping a daily record, constructing dialogues with ourselves, our families, and our friends. See especially Chapter 11, "Time Stretching. Moving

Back and Forward in Our Life History. Reconstructing
Our Autobiography."

THE POLISH AMERICAN FAMILY

Greeley, Andrew M. *The American Catholic: A Social
Portrait.* **New York: Basic Books, 1977.**

Includes discussions of the family patterns of Polish
Americans, the behavior of first- and second-generation
Polish Americans, parochial education, political behavior,
racial attitudes, and politics. Contains several informative
tables.

Hareven, Tamara K. *Family Time and Industrial
Time: The Relationship Between the Family and Work
in a New England Industrial Community.* **New York:
Cambridge University Press, 1982.**

Specific references to Polish Americans.

**Mindel, Charles H.; Habenstein, Robert W.; and
Wright, Roosevelt, Jr., eds.** *Ethnic Families in
America: Patterns and Variations,* **3d ed. New York:
Elsevier, 1988.**

See Chapter 2, "The Polish American Family," and the
bibliography attached to the article.

**Polzin, Theresita. "The Polish American Family—I:
The Sociological Aspects of the Families of Polish
Immigrants to America before World War II, and
Their Descendants."** *Polish Review,* **Vol. 21, 1976, pp.
103–122.**

For readers interested in a sociological perspective. Polzin
examines the emergence of a second generation of Polish
Americans. Second-generation Polish Americans often
experience conflict between their parents' "old-world"
values and American values.

Sanders, Irwin, T. *Polish-American Community Life: A Survey of Research.* **Boston: Polish Institute of Arts and Sciences of America, 1975.**

Chapters on the residential patterns and ethnic segregation of Polish Americans, the structural position of Polish Americans in American society, political participation and interethnic relations, the church and the community, the family, social relations, culture, and ethnic identity and identification. Extensive bibliography.

Thomas, John L. *The American Catholic Family.* **Englewood Cliffs, NJ: Prentice-Hall, 1956.**

References to Polish Catholic immigrants, their ethnic solidarity, marital maladjustment problems, and out-group marriages.

Chapter 7
Your Kin Group or Family

Genealogical and family research may provoke certain questions about what anthropologists call kinship. The "biological" family—parents and their children—is the dominant group in our society, but more and more people live in families of a different composition. In all families, there may have been generations or periods when the household lacked a father or a mother, or when a home seemed to revolve around an older brother or sister, uncle, aunt, cousin, or grandparents. Part of the Polish American experience may encompass times when the mother or father parented alone. Because of work patterns, health or economic problems, or a family's size, it is also not unusual for older brothers or sisters to have raised their younger siblings.

Reading about kinship in other societies may help highlight how Polish American families have functioned. Certain aspects of a Polish American heritage may then stand out. In studying a particular family, think about how closely it has been tied to its community. Did the Church serve as an important socializing force? (See John L. Thomas, *The American Catholic Family,* in the **Resources** of Chapter 6.) Did the family participate in the community through church activities? Was parochial school a regular part of the family's educational experience? To what extent, in other words, has the Polish American family defined itself by the institutions that the Polish community has established to assist its adaptation to American life? Or has a family moved away from traditional Polish American institutions? How has its attempt to define itself influenced different family members? Has the family been inner-directed, relying essentially on a small group of close relatives? Or are there examples of family members participating in organizations that take the family out of its own neighborhood sphere and encourage a broader engagement with other communities?

Thinking in sociological and historical categories may also provide additional perspective on the Polish American family. Is it working class (blue-collar) or middle class (white-collar)? Understanding how family members have behaved within class and kinship categories will also reveal their Polish American experience, their desire to remain close to their ethnic background or to broaden it.

Traditional Polish Families

Study how the family has perpetuated (perhaps without realizing it) patterns prevalent in family life in Poland. The form of the family, especially in rural regions of the country, tended to be patriarchal, dominated by a father. In peasant society, the father often kept his sons near him and exercised considerable power and authority over all his children. The father also designated his heir, the son who would take the father's place as the family authority. Such patterns have relaxed in the United States, yet Polish American families may exhibit vestiges of this traditional family organization.

Investigate how many family stems are linked to the nuclear family, a stem meaning an offshoot of the family progenitor listed in the family tree. Have his sons and daughters created families still linked to each other, creating an extensive chain of kinship? Has the family become a kind of clan, related to each other by descent from a common progenitor? Have others (friends of the family) become part of what might be called your adoptive kinship network?

Consider to what extent relatives by marriage (rather than by bloodline) have contributed to the family history. A stepmother or stepfather may constitute an important factor in family study. Previous generations may yield similar important relatives by marriage. They may show how the family has enlarged and enriched itself at crucial moments in its adaptation to the United States.

Death, divorce, and marital separations have a significant

impact on a family. Some of the readings below explore sensitive and troubling events in family life, providing a context for understanding how individuals relate to each other in difficult situations. Problems in family cohesion can be disturbing, but they may also have resulted in successful efforts to overcome disruptions of home and work life.

Adjustment to the United States

Because most Polish immigrants came from rural communities and were rapidly thrust into modern, urban, industrialized environments, it was predicted that there would be widespread family disorganization. But as John L. Thomas points out in *The American Catholic Family*, the immigrants steadied themselves with their parish organizations and strong religious faith. First and second generations stayed together, seldom marrying into other ethnic groups.

In considering the nature of the Polish American family, consult the classic study *The Polish Peasant*, by William I. Thomas and Florian Znaniecki (see the **Resources** section in Chapter 1). It will give you a framework for thinking about the origins of the Polish American family. Thomas and Znaniecki speculated that peasant psychology would make it difficult for immigrants to become modern Americans. How would they form new social ideals unrelated to their previous lives? How could the institution of marriage survive, since immigrant women would be forced to work and thus undermine male authority? The patriarchal structure of peasant society could not survive, and the new immigrants would find themselves lacking a center of meaning. Disenchanted and demoralized Polish men would not be able to improve their economic position, lacking both the education and the motivation to compete for better, increasingly sophisticated jobs.

Thomas and Znaniecki vastly exaggerated the problems of Polish immigrants because they did not sufficiently take into account subjective factors: the personal feelings of immigrants, their dreams and hopes, their fierce determination to succeed. Each immigrant had a story to tell, a kind of script

Most early Polish immigrants came from rural communities, but they were able to adjust to life in large American cities by forming strong communities with the Church as a unifying force.

for his or her life that the United States was destined to complete.

Finally, Thomas and Znaniecki exaggerated the Polish immigrant as a type: a peasant rigidly bound by the structures of his or her European upbringing. Polish immigrants proved remarkably flexible, incorporating American values and gradually modifying many of their old-country beliefs to suit their new land. The family and the Church, for example, provided continuity. Like Italian Americans, Polish Americans tended to cherish the value of the extended family, building intricate networks of blood relationships that helped individuals to succeed.

John Bodnar's *Workers' World* (Chapter 4 **Resources**) is an apt title for a book that triumphantly demonstrates how immigrant families took charge of their lives, establishing their own institutions and kinship ties. Before the large-scale unionization of the working class in the 1930s, Polish

Americans and other ethnic groups concentrated on an ethic of self-improvement, ensuring that their children, if not themselves, became literate. Immigrants promoted an ideology of advancement; they expected life to get better for themselves and their children, if only they worked and studied hard enough. All of this was to be done as a family. As Bodnar observes of his interviews with Polish Americans, the family base was crucial. Individuals felt both obligated and responsible for their families; good family reputations meant getting jobs, for example, in Pittsburgh neighborhoods. Often family members refused to leave family and neighborhood out of a deep sense of loyalty. Not that family members did not resist or dislike conforming to family goals, but they found it difficult, and sometimes impossible, to consider only their individual welfare. Finding jobs, keeping jobs, locating housing—all were dependent on an individual's kinship ties.

In fact, as Bodnar points out, work and family were not distinct categories; rather, there developed an "enclave" in which the experiences of Polish life and labor melded. Enclaves became communities of industrial workers, in which ethnicity, skill, and shared economic status were the bases on which families commingled, intermarried, and became self-sufficient. In general, they operated as an enclave that cut itself off from wider social and political activities and institutions. In the enclave, families shared their consciousness of isolation and knew that their strength depended on solidifying their kinship ties. Especially before the New Deal in the 1930s, before the introduction of large-scale social programs that helped the poor and laws that protected labor unions, Polish Americans—like other immigrant groups— instilled family loyalty in family members who knew they could expect relatively little help from outside the family.

Thus, children learned work skills from their parents; sons were apprenticed to fathers or to other close relatives. Family was the individual's livelihood, and his or her self-esteem derived from the family's approval. In this workers' world, families concerned themselves with immediate, everyday problems. They concentrated on establishing good relations with the foreman in a factory. It was not an unusual practice for a Polish immigrant to find easier, less laborious jobs by cultivating his supervisors or finding relatives who would give him a good reference. Of course, the power of immigrants and the children of immigrants in the workplace was strictly limited, and it varied greatly from Pittsburgh's steel plants, to Pennsylvania's coal mines, to Detroit's automobile factories. When families migrated within the United States, it was often to higher-paying, cleaner, and less arduous work. Assembly-line labor in an automobile factory was repetitive and boring, but it seemed an improvement over the sweaty, grimy shifts in steel plants.

The 1930s accelerated Polish assimilation because it involved organizing industrial workers on a national scale. The Great Depression represented an unprecedented threat to local, family-based enclaves. Small communities simply could not cope with the huge economic dislocations, the closing down of businesses, factories, and banks. Nevertheless, families were not superseded as a principle of Polish American life; rather, they were incorporated into union organizing activities, which became part of the effort to preserve families at all costs. Friends and families actually enhanced kinship ties by joining unions together, making sure that the whole family participated in the organization's activities. In some cases, Polish immigrants and their children challenged their employers' power, gradually earning better working conditions and fairer wages. Although the nature of the enclave had to change, that change was a natural extension of the determination of Polish Americans to thrive in a new land. The very changes made in the enclave perpetuated its continuity.

John Bodnar has argued that deeply conservative tendencies have always informed the lives of working-class immigrants and their children. Participation in unionization and drives for social, political, and economic reform can be interpreted as ways to maintain and fortify the family, which is to say that kinship ties have been the most strongly motivating factor at work and at home. Even as society changed,

Polish Americans, like other immigrant groups, sought to retain what was familiar. "The integrity of the worker's world came first," Bodnar concludes.

Polish Americans fared well in an industrial setting. By 1900, almost all of the 3,000 employees of Detroit's Peninsular Car Company were Polish. By 1909, Polish women dominated Chicago's restaurant and kitchen jobs. By 1911, 65 percent of Poles were in manufacturing and mechanical jobs compared to 28.8 percent of Southern Italians. This clustering of Poles was due, in part, to kinship ties, although it was also attributable to the skills Polish immigrants brought wth them to the United States. After 1900, unskilled Polish laborers relied on relatives to find them jobs in entry-level positions in factories, and industrial managers often abetted this concentration of Polish Americans and other ethnic groups, believing that Poles, for example, were better in indoor factory and mill jobs, whereas Italians excelled in outdoor work. These labor practices served to reinforce the immigrant's sense of family and worker identity.

Of course, there were Polish Americans who left their community, established their own businesses, and abandoned the enclave mentality. Many families also had members who straddled the enclave and the larger American society by attaining higher education or marrying outside their ethnic group. Polish American women sometimes married outside their ethnic and kinship group. World War II enhanced the position of many Polish American women, who suddenly found themselves able to work in factories. Many women were forced to give up these jobs to returning servicemen after the war, but their attitudes toward their families and their sense of themselves greatly changed and sometimes weakened their enclave mentality.

When constructing a family history, consider not only this historical development of the immigrant community and its second- and third-generation descendants, but the extent to which the family exhibited its role in the enclave by attending family and community picnics, weddings, and other social activities. Each family's character derives from this kinship tradition, but each family member has reacted in his or her own way to kinship ties, strengthening the enclave, but also, in many cases, broadening it to include a larger community as subsequent generations become assimilated into the larger fabric of American life.

In Carl Rollyson's Polish American family, for example, his grandfather's two sons (Carl's uncles) responded to the larger society quite differently. One uncle graduated from college and adopted his father's shortened Polish name, Sokolik, whereas another uncle never finished high school, worked in automobile factories, and quite proudly clung to the family name, Sokolnicki. Yet no one in the family was more pleased with Carl's decision to attend college than his uncle who had comparatively little schooling. These two uncles had quite different personalities; yet when it came to family and the desire to see everyone in it prosper, everyone saw the next generation as a continued investment in the United States.

In reviewing the history of the Polish American family and perhaps studying your own, you may be struck by how different the family appears today. Does it still function as a mini-enclave? Or has it been dispersed, moving away from urban and rural communities to suburban, less ethnically oriented neighborhoods? What were the events that led to this changing concept of the family? Are there key episodes that should be highlighted in a family history? Do certain family members stand out as altering the family's sense of itself?

If you come from a single-parent family of Polish American heritage, or if you are not biologically related to your family, your genealogical search or family history may be defined slightly differently from what you have read in conventional books on the subject. You may even wish to begin with your immediate family, gradually enlarging your study to include friends and kin who make up the support network of your life. Whatever you choose to do, you have a tremendous opportunity not merely to discover the roots of the family that matters to you, but also to create meaning in your life and in the lives of those who mean the most to you.

Resources

Adams, Bert N. *Kinship in an Urban Setting*. Chicago: Markham Publishing Co., 1968.

The introduction is somewhat difficult because of its scholarly terms, but the glossary helps with the reading and also provides key terms that may help in organizing a family history.

Bayer, Alan E. *The Assimilation of American Family Patterns by European Immigrants and Their Children*. New York: Arno Press, 1980.

Chapters on immigration laws, different immigrant groups (age, sex, marriage, and family factors), occupational variation, and differences in rural and urban settings. Contains many detailed tables of data.

Boatright, Mody C.; Downs, Robert B.; and Flanagan, John T. *The Family Saga and Other Phases of American Folklore*. Urbana: University of Illinois Press, 1958.

In Chapter 1, "The Family Saga as a Form of Folklore," Boatright explores how and why families develop their own history. She estimates that over a million people are at work on such histories.

Brown, Gene, ed. *The Family*. New York: Arno Press, 1979.

A compilation of newspaper articles on family from 1870 to the 1960s, emphasizing family relationships, changes in women's rights, the institution of marriage, the impact of the Depression, World War II, changes in parental roles, and more.

Gordon, Michael, ed. *The American Family in Social-Historical Perspective.* **New York: St. Martin's Press, 1973.**

An important introduction to the study of family history. Divided into five sections, each covering a different aspect of family and kinship.

Gronowicz, Antoni. *Bolek.* **New York: Thomas Nelson and Sons, 1942.**

This novel is a comprehensive portrayal of Polish and American kinship. Explores the experiences of Poles in Chicago and Pittsburgh and evokes the Poles' sense of America as the promised land.

Lasch, Christopher. *Haven in a Heartless World: The Family Besieged.* **New York: Basic Books, 1977.**

Chapter 1 is a provocative discussion of the making of the modern family.

Macklin, Eleanor D., and Rubin, Roger H., eds. *Contemporary Families and Alternative Lifestyles: Handbook on Research and Theory.* **Beverly Hills, CA: Sage Publications, 1983.**

Chapters 12 and 14 cover "Contemporary Traditional Families: The Undefined Majority" and "The Present and Future of Alternative Lifestyles in Ethnic American Families." Contains a bibliography.

McGinnis, Thomas C., and Ginnegan, Dana G. *Open Family and Marriage: A Guide to Personal Growth.* **Saint Louis: C. V. Mosby Company, 1976.**

The early chapters have a useful discussion of family life in the early 1900s.

Modell, Judith. *Kinship with Strangers: Adoption and Interpretations of Kinship in American Culture.* **Berkeley: University of California Press, 1994.**

Chapters on the history of American adoption, birth parents' experiences of adoption, growing up adopted, the adoptee's search for a birth family, the birth parent's search for an adopted child, and how the changes in adoption policy are affecting attitudes toward kinship. Includes an extensive bibliography.

Perin, Constance. *Belonging in America: Reading Between the Lines*. **Madison: University of Wisconsin Press, 1988.**

A provocative exploration of the meaning of family and community, with sections on "drawing family lines," "converting friends to family," "parenting people," and "the constitution of men and women." Contains a bibliography.

Pincus, Lily, and Dare, Christopher. *Secrets in the Family*. **New York: Pantheon Books, 1978.**

The prologue, "Secrets in the Life Cycle of the Family," discusses the myths that develop in a family, the relationship between these myths and the facts, and how these myths are carried from one generation to another.

Sanders, Irwin T., and Morawska, Ewa T. *Polish-American Community Life: A Survey of Research*. **Vol. II. Boston: Boston University, Department of Sociology, 1975.**

Chapters on residential patterns and ethnic segregation, the structural position of Polish Americans in American society, political participation and interethnic relations, the church and the community, organization affiliation, the family, social relations, culture, and ethnic identity and identification. Comprehensive bibliography of Polish American and other Polonian Community Studies.

Shell, Marc. *Children of the Earth: Literature, Politics, and Nationhood*. **New York: Oxford University Press, 1993.**

A fascinating study of how different societies establish kinship and family. Recommended for advanced readers, and for those wishing to take a very broad view of family history. Extensive notes and bibliography.

Sussman, Marvin B., and Steinmetz, Suzanne K. *Handbook of Marriage and the Family*. New York: Plenum Press, 1987.

An excellent reference work for considering the development of families and the roles of family members. Discusses "Historical Analysis of the Family," "Social Stratification" (with comments on immigrant families), "Families and Work," "Families and Religions," "Nontraditional Family Forms," "Single-Parent Families," and "Divorce."

Thorne, Barrie, and Yalom, Marilyn, eds. *Rethinking the Family: Some Feminist Questions*. New York: Longman, 1982.

Somewhat difficult for nonscholars but helpful in thinking about new ways in which focusing on women redefines family life and history.

Weston, Kath. *Families We Chose: Lesbians, Gays, Kinship*. New York: Columbia University Press, 1991.

A vivid, lively study of gay and lesbian families, especially valuable for its numerous accounts of individual families, with anecdotes and narratives that provide models of how to tell the history of nontraditional families. Includes a statistical appendix on nontraditional families, extensive notes, and bibliography.

Wilkes, Paul. *Six American Families*. New York: Seabury/Parthenon Press Books, 1977.

Chapter 2 is on "The Pasciak Family of Chicago."

Chapter 8
Tracing Your Roots If You Are Adopted

Searching for your roots, if you are an adopted child, requires a special set of skills; it also demands great sensitivity. Consider not only your own feelings, but those of your adoptive family and of your birth parents. Ask yourself why you want to trace your roots. It is the most natural thing in the world, of course, to want to know where you came from, what your ethnic background is, who you look like. But imagine the impact on you and others when you pursue these questions. Adoptive parents often look upon adoption as a rebirth for the child. At adoption proceedings, a new birth certificate is issued, replacing the names of birth parents with those of the adoptive parents, and the legal relationship between birth parents and child is terminated. In most cases, records are then sealed, so that the identities of the birth parents are kept confidential. Not even the adoptee is given access.

In the last three decades, this closing of birth records has been challenged by adoptees and organizations working for adoptees' rights, who argue for the right to know one's birth parents for both psychological and medical reasons. Until the 1960s, adoptees had very few rights when it came to obtaining knowledge about their origins. Most laws mandated a complete break between the adoptee's original family and his or her new one. The open-adoption movement has successfully challenged some of those laws, but government agencies remain reluctant to open sealed records.

As Margaret O. Hyde points out in *Foster Care and Adoption* (see **Resources** section), "some adoptees search long and hard to find the mothers who gave them birth." She tells several stories of adoptees who must weigh the desire to

find their birth parents against the possibility that they will
hurt their adoptive parents' feelings. Sometimes one adoptive parent is more sympathetic than the other to the
adoptee's questions. Often the way an adoptee's questions
are phrased can either set the adoptive parents at ease or
make them uncomfortable. In Chapter 7, "Searching for
Roots," Hyde presents the case of Paul, who confides in his
adoptive parents and sets off in quest of his birth mother.
Hyde presents a vivid description of Paul's search through
court records, his interviews with a courthouse clerk, his
travels to Chicago to check nurses' registries, his study of his
medical records (which yielded the fact that his mother had
married). Hyde also shows that Paul himself begins to have
second thoughts. Is he ready to meet his birth mother? Has
she remained married? What other changes have there been
in her life? He learns that his birth mother does not want to
resume a relationship with him, but both of them have an
opportunity to share feelings they have concealed for a long
time. Paul realizes he will never see her again, yet he gains a
better understanding of why she put him up for adoption.

In other cases, birth parents welcome reunions; indeed,
birth parents may have been searching for the children who
find them. For some birth parents, the reunion with their
children is an opportunity to relieve themselves of guilt and
shame and to explain to their children why they had to give
them up. Some searches for birth parents and children never
end. It is important to realize just how difficult both the
search and the reunion with birth parents can be.

An adoptee's search may be no different from that of
children who know who their birth parents are. He or she
may choose simply to consider the adoptive parents as birth
parents and research the adoptive family history.

A search for birth parents requires persistence, patience,
and tact. Family members may think it is best not to dig up
the past. Respect their feelings while explaining your own
goals and feelings. Your search may bring you closer to your
adoptive family; it may forge a new relationship with your
birth parents.

The **Resources** section of this chapter provides a sampling of the current literature on adoptees' searches for their biological parents. A reading of this literature suggests that you need to carefully consider how you will conduct your search and what your goals are. How much do *you* need to know? How will you handle your search? Do you want to meet your birth parents, or is it simply the knowledge of your origins that most interests you? How will you make your adoptive parents a part of your search? Will you welcome help from them? Will they feel threatened by your search?

Spend some time thinking of nonthreatening approaches to the family members you wish to contact and perhaps to interview. Perhaps a brief letter stating your concerns would be the best approach. Enclose a photograph of yourself. Say something about your interests, gradually showing your interviewee who you are and what you are like. Most important of all, you have to convince everyone that the reason for tracing your roots is to add value, not to take it away. You are not simply acquiring information; you are sharing and increasing it.

It may help you in your search if you avoid certain phrases such as "finding my family." As Jayne Askin, the author of a handbook for adoptees and birth parents, points out, such language may offend an adoptive family, who believe the adoptee has a family and does not need a new one. Explain that you are searching for a sense of connection with the past. In this respect, your question is no different from that of anyone doing a genealogical search. Jayne Askin also counsels against using the term "natural parents" to refer to biological parents. The term implies that adoptive parents are somehow unnatural, or illegitimate, or artificial. Askin's advice shows just how sensitive you will have to be to other people's feelings. You may mean no harm, you may not intend to be insulting, yet your choice of words may offend your adoptive family. Some tension may be unavoidable; you may misread your adoptive family's feelings. Do not be surprised if you do. Above all, try not to feel hurt yourself.

Throughout the stages of your search, it will be helpful to have a group of friends, family members, or perhaps an adoptees' support organization that can counsel you or just share their own experiences of searching for birth parents. The worst thing is to isolate yourself. Feelings of rejection and failure are probably inescapable, but they do not have to dominate your search if you realize that there are people who have experienced the same thing and who are interested in helping you.

Remember that the basics of the search—how to access records and papers—are similar to what other genealogical researchers need to master. You may actually find that the discipline of becoming a researcher is therapeutic, allowing you to gain some perspective on your birth and adoptive families. In fact, you should also include your adoptive family in your search for roots, since they have helped to create the environment you live in and the history that encompasses you.

Even if you do not accomplish all the goals of your search, you will undoubtedly learn more about yourself—at the same time sharpening your sense of family and community. As with any genealogical search, you will master many skills and learn about many different sources of information from librarians, government officials, and professionals. As an adoptee, you may also form contacts with search and support groups.

Perhaps you will conclude that genealogy, or the making of a family tree, is not the point of your search. Or that your bond with your adoptive parents is one that you need to center on and celebrate. Who we are is not merely a matter of bloodlines and pedigrees; we are also the products of a culture and community. Adoptive parents are often keenly aware of passing on to the next generation certain values and traditions, and it is these customs and mores that may become the focus of a family history.

Resources

Adamec, Christine, and Pierce, William L. *The Encyclopedia of Adoption*. **New York: Facts on File, 1991.**

The introduction provides a brief history of adoption. Entries are arranged A–Z and supply explanation of key terms such as "adopted away/adopted in" (legal terminology referring to a child and his or her birth family and a child entering the adoptive family), organizations such as the American Adoption Congress, and a range of records and services. Many entries include bibliographies and addresses. The appendix also provides important addresses, statistics, and additional bibliography.

Askin, Jayne, with Molly Davis. *Search: A Handbook for Adoptees and Birth Parents*, **2nd ed. Phoenix, AZ: Oryx Press, 1992.**

A detailed introduction to searching for birth parents, including chapters on the costs of searching; reference resources in government institutions, libraries, and genealogical societies; state and federal laws governing adoption; instructions on how to access primary data such as hospital and agency records, records for black-market babies; alternative sources of information, such as newspaper and magazine ads; search and support groups, family reunion registries; hiring researchers and acquiring legal assistance; a reading list of adoption-related books and articles.

Fisher, Florence. *The Search for Anna Fisher*. **New York: Arthur Fields Books, 1973.**

An account of an adopted child and her search for her parents. She describes her efforts to contact other adoptees, and her meeting with her birth father. It is also a story of how the search affected her identity.

Gediman, Judith S., and Brown, Linda P. *BirthBond: Reunions Between Birthparents and Adoptees—What Happens After . . .* Far Hills, NJ: New Horizon Press, 1989.

Several stories of reunions between adoptees and birth parents; separate chapters on why reunions happen and what happens afterward, on birth fathers, siblings, birth mothers, and adoptive parents. Includes notes, bibliography, and adoption, reunion, and postreunion resources.

Hyde, Margaret O. *Foster Care and Adoption.* New York: Franklin Watts, 1982.

Chapter 7 discusses "Searching for Roots." Includes bibliography and sources of further information, which lists several organizations such as "Adoptees in Search," "Adoptees Liberty Movement Association," "Orphan Voyage," and "Parent Finders."

Klibanoff, Susan, and Klibanoff, Elton. *Let's Talk About Adoption.* Boston: Little, Brown, 1973.

A good introduction to the subject, beginning with a chapter by Susan Klibanoff with a "mother's-eye view" of her own decision to adopt. Appendixes include information on adoptive parents' groups, model bylaws of an adoptive parents' organization, and model reform laws pertaining to the rights of both biological parents and adoptive children.

Lifton, Betty Jean. *Journey of the Adopted Self: A Quest for Wholeness.* New York: Basic Books, 1994.

An adopted child herself, Lifton has divided her book into three parts that mirror the phases of the adoptee's psychological development: The Self in Crisis, The Self in Search, The Self in Transformation. She includes a valuable "Resources" section.

————. *Lost and Found: The Adoption Experience.* **New York: Dial Press, 1979.**

Part 1 focuses on the psychology of the adoptee from childhood to adulthood. Part 2 concentrates on how adoptees decide to search for their birth parents, stages of the search, varieties of the reunion experience, what happens after the reunion, and the roles of fathers, siblings, and wives of adoptees. Part 3 deals with the adoptee's relationship with adoptive parents. Includes information on adoptee search groups.

Maxtone-Graham, Katrina. *An Adopted Woman.* New York: Remi Books, 1983.

The story of her search for her birth parents, beginning with the agency from which she was adopted and going on to her reunion with her mother and her search for her father.

McKuen, Rod. *Finding My Father: One Man's Search for Identity.* New York: Coward, McCann & Geoghegan, 1976.

The popular poet describes his involvement in a television program on adoptees that spurred his own search for his father. An insightful view of the adoptee's psychology and the significance of the search for birth parents.

Powledge, Fred. *So You're Adopted.* New York: Charles Scribner's Sons, 1982.

Chapters on how adoption has changed, the statistics of adoption, how the adopted child develops, the adult adoptee, and searching for roots ("why, when, who"). Contains a bibliography.

Sachdev, Paul. *Unlocking the Adoption Files.* Lexington, MA: Lexington Books, 1989.

A book about the "adoption rectangle—adoptive parents, birth mothers, adoptees, and social work personnel—and their attitudes toward opening adoption records." Perhaps the first chapter will be most helpful for beginning researchers; other chapters are highly technical and of most use to scholars and those interested in changing laws governing adoption.

Sorosky, Arthur D.; Baran, Annette; and Pannor, Reuben. *The Adoption Triangle: The Effects of the Sealed Record on Adoptees, Birth Parents, and Adoptive Parents.* **Garden City, NY: Doubleday, 1978.**

See the three chapters on the adoptee: childhood, adolescence, adulthood, and on the search for and reunion with birth parents. Contains a bibliography.

Triseliotis, John. *In Search of Origins: The Experiences of Adopted People.* **Boston: Routledge & Kegan Paul, 1973.**

Chapters cover the perception of family relationships, self-perception and identity, why search now, hopes and expectations, the search and after. Contains a bibliography.

Wishard, Laurie, and Wishard, William R. *Adoption: The Grafted Tree.* **San Francisco: Cragmont Publications, 1979.**

Part 1 concentrates on the decision to seek out birth parents. Other chapters discuss parents, the legal process, the adoptive family. Includes an appendix on adoption resources and a glossary.

Conclusion

As in a genealogical search or family history, we come to an end and it is really only a beginning. What this book has shown, and what your own search will reveal, is that you are part of a lifecycle. Tracing your roots always brings you around again to yourself. You will see yourself or other family members in the faces and in the traces of your family's past. At the same time, you should also recognize your individuality, and that it is precisely the ways in which you differ from family members that will probably enrich the family, bringing it new resources and possibilities. You tread in your search, in other words, between the future and the past.

This book has suggested many different kinds of projects. You can be a historian, an autobiographer, an interviewer, a fiction writer, a photographer, or a biographer. Each project develops different but complementary skills, encouraging you to try out different roles. Above all, the making of family trees, oral histories, and other kinds of albums of experience turns you into an interpreter, analyst, and creator.

Through excursions to cemeteries, libraries, courthouses, and perhaps to the "old country," you will meet many fascinating people. You will also be bringing your family's history to the world, claiming a place for your family as your own progenitors did in earlier generations.

The story of immigration is the American story; it is America's past and its future. By telling your part of it, you help to complete the story, rounding out a sense of yourself in the process.

Glossary

ancestor   One from whom an individual is descended.

anti-Semitism   Hostility toward Jews as a minority.

archives   Organized body of records; a repository of evidence.

assimilation   The immigrant's absorption into the prevailing or mainstream American culture.

communism   Common ownership of property; a government in which a single party rules, specifically a form of government established by the Russian Revolution in 1917 and maintained by Vladimir Lenin and his successors. Lenin followed the teachings of Karl Marx (1818–1883), who believed that Communist states would replace Capitalists. Some of Marx's followers, including Lenin, advocated world revolution. The United States and other Western nations opposed the Soviet Union by adopting the policy of containment.

data   Information organized for purposes of analysis.

displaced persons   Large numbers of people who, because of their nationality, religion, race, or political convictions, have been expelled from their homeland. A term used most widely to describe refugees who settled in the United States after World War II.

dissenters   Those who disagree with commonly held opinions or who may protest the policies of a group such as a government or church.

emigrate   To leave one country or region to settle in another.

enclave   A culturally distinct unit within a foreign territory.

ethnic group   A group of people sharing common traits and customs.

family tree A chart or diagram of the descent of a family, showing how various branches are related to each other.

genealogy A record or table of descent of a family, group, or person from an ancestor or ancestors; a lineage; the study of family histories.

genogram A family tree that emphasizes both genealogical and psychological relationships and significant family events.

gender The classification of sex, male or female.

ghetto A quarter of a city inhabited by members of a minority group who reside there for reasons of social, legal, or economic pressure.

Holocaust The killing of European Jews by the Nazis during World War II.

immigrate To enter and settle in a country or region to which one is not native.

kinship The state of being related by common ancestry.

nontraditional Applied to families, it refers to any family-like arrangement that does not have both a mother and father.

nuclear family Mother, father, and children.

extended family Grandparents and other relatives.

Partition The division of Poland into separate lands ruled by Austria, Prussia, and Russia.

Polonia The community of Polish Americans.

Solidarity An independent labor union, led by Lech Walesa, that challenged Poland's Communist government and whose ranks grew to include both workers and intellectuals.

source A person, book, document—anything that supplies information.

Index

Q

questionnaire, family
members, 102
questions, sequence of,
113–115

R

records, 94
census, 96, 101
church, 94, 99
military, 7, 93, 98
Polish, 96–97
tax, 111
relationship, gender,
129
roots, tracing, 1, 8, 98,
101, 140, 156–159
Rubinstein, Helena, 46
Russia, 6, 35, 37

S

scrapbook, 99, 133, 136,
139
secrets, family, 136
self-discovery, 7
Shalikashvili, John, 3
Slovakia, 35
software programs, 138
Solidarity, 43, 45, 62–
67, 139

sources, information, 93
Soviet Union, 35, 40,
42, 45
State Archives, Polish,
97
steel plants, 39, 149
subject file, family
members, 93–94,
98
subsystems, family,
130
support organization,
adoptees', 159
surname, 92, 97, 102
Swit, Loretta, 46
synagogue, 94

T

tape recorder, 115, 117
Terkel, Studs, 138
Teutonic Knights, 35
Thomas, John L., 146
Thomas, William D.,
146–147
tradition, oral, 134

U

Ukraine, 35
United States, 42

V

videotape, 138
vital records, 94, 97

W

Waffen SS, 3
Walesa, Lech, 43, 62–67
Warsaw Ghetto, 43,
55–62
Washington, DC, 101
Westin, Jeane Eddy,
101–102, 103
Wisconsin, 6
women, working outside
the home, 39, 146,
150
World War I, 40
World War II, 40, 42, 150

Y

Yaztrzemski, Carl, 46

Z

Znaniecki, Florian, 146–
147

ABOUT THE AUTHORS

Carl Sokolnicki Rollyson is a professor of English at Baruch College, The City University of New York. He has published six biographies and several articles on Poland and Eastern Europe. **Lisa Olson Paddock** is a lawyer and a free-lance writer. She has published books and essays on literature and the law.

ILLUSTRATION CREDITS

Cover, © Steven Kosek; cover inset, From the Permanent Collection of the Kosciuszko Foundation, Inc.; pp. 2, 4, 5, 7, 36, 38, 40, 41, 44, 95, 100, 114, 116, 120, 135, 137, 140, 147, BETTMAN. *Color insert:* p. 2, W. T. Benda, *Krakowiak* (From the Permanent Collection of the Kosciuszko Foundation, Inc.); p. 3, From the Permanent Collection of the Kosciuszko Foundation, Inc.; p. 4, Joseph Bagrowski, *City Hall, Baltimore, Maryland* (From the Permanent Collection of the Kosciuszko Foundation, Inc.); p. 5, S. Zaloga, *Polish Church, Adams, MA* (From the Permanent Collection of the Kosciuszko Foundation, Inc.), p. 6, David Chou, *Young Polish Gentleman in Parade* (From the Permanent Collection of the Kosciuszko Foundation, Inc.); p. 7, Ralph Carrano, *Pulaski Day Parade* (From the Permanent Collection of the Kosciuszko Foundation, Inc.); p. 8, BETTMAN; p. 9, © Catherine Smith/Impact Visuals; pp. 10, 11, 12, 13, 14, 15, 16, BETTMAN.

LAYOUT AND DESIGN

Kim Sonsky